A Great
New Way
to Make
Money

Also by the author

How I Turn Ordinary Complaints into Thousands of Dollars

A Great New Way to Make Money

---

51 CONSECUTIVE
PROFITS IN
5 MONTHS

Ralph Charell

STEIN AND DAY/*Publishers*/New York

First published in 1976
Copyright © 1976 by Ralph Charell
All rights reserved
Designed by Ed Kaplin
Printed in the United States of America
Stein and Day/*Publishers*/Scarborough House,
Briarcliff Manor, N.Y. 10510

Library of Congress Cataloging in Publication Data

Charell, Ralph.
    A great new way to make money.

    1. Investments.   2. Put and call options.
I. Title.
HG4527.C47   332.6 78   75-11783
ISBN 0-8128-1826-1

Contents

A Great
New Way
to Make
Money

1. Taking Off

I grew up on the movies of the thirties and forties and they almost ruined my life. It was easy to identify with all of the nice-guy protagonists. Jimmy Stewart, Gary Cooper, Hank Fonda, and the other good guys were my kind of people. For years, I received the same message from big screens in darkened theaters: "Even if it looks hopeless, if you do what's right, everything will work out perfectly in the end." I, of course, along with millions of other innocents, bought the idea of sure things and happy endings.

A kid I knew, whose family was on hard times in the late thirties, located and memorized the proper forms of address to royalty, so that if he were ever invited to Buckingham Palace he wouldn't act like a klutz. Had we been born ten years later, our attitudes would have been a lot closer to the mark. Italian neo-realism and other harsher, post-World War II portrayals of the world during our formative years would have made the difference. We undoubtedly would have learned that happy endings are not guaranteed, a simple fact that eluded me until I was about twenty-five.

When I moved into the commercial world, probably my biggest deficiency was that I didn't realize you had to *do* anything to assure a favorable outcome. After all, those movie actors with whom I had identified all those years really hadn't done very much. They were simply good guys and everything fell into place for them in the last reel. As I, too, was a good guy it seemed to me that all I required was patience. It was easy to believe in magic.

But the magic didn't work so well in daylight. Even great patience was often unrewarded. The long, slow relearning process began.

Many, many years later, almost by accident, long after my belief in magic had been forced into the deepest recesses of memory (but not abandoned), I actually stumbled upon one of the magic formulas I'd sought so earnestly as a child. The feeling was indescribable. It was as if I'd gone on a camping trip to the North Pole, just to get away from it all, and suddenly, as I approached the crest of a snowy rise, a man in a red suit with a long white beard came into view.

"It can't be," I gasped. "You're not . . . "

"Ho, ho, ho" replied the jolly fat man. "It is and I am."

Whereupon he invited me to meet the missus, showed me where he made all the toys, and let me feed the reindeer.

Well, I had the same kind of unreal feeling when I realized that there was actually a way to turn a fairly modest investment into a handsome nest egg and with a safety and certainty I'd only dreamed of, in the new, listed options markets.

My first impulse was to tell my friends (who would tell their friends) and then to publish it and let everybody into the tent. After I'd taken seven consecutive profits with my new approach, I was sure I was on to something. I wrote to my publisher and suggested this book. But he knew that before people would listen, you first had to get their attention, as the old joke has it. We agreed that I would take fifty-one consecutive profits before the book went to press. At even money on each trade ,° the odds against fifty-one straight profits without a single loss were 1,125,899,-599,999,999 to 1, more than one and one-eighth quadrillion to one against me. To put this number into perspective, if four billion men, women, and children each tried this feat 281,475 times, the odds are that only one of them would succeed once.

We thought these long odds would tend to validate the method and eliminate luck and accident as likely reasons for success. It took several months, but the assignment was finally completed (as is documented in detail in the following pages) and without the help of Rumpelstiltskin. And just to show you that I'm still the same nice guy I was as a kid, you're about to be let in on the "magic formula."

But first a few words of caution. Please do not risk a penny on the basis of a quick scanning of what I've done, or on a vague and incomplete notion of how to proceed. Do not experiment with real money until you've tried it out on paper successfully at least a few times. It is absolutely necessary that you get the feeling of the trades before you consider trading with hard-earned money.

If and when you do begin to trade with real money, do not overcommit your funds. Don't risk a large proportion of your cash on any one trade, and don't use funds you cannot afford to lose. Protect yourself at all times. There are

---

° Nobody really knows the precise odds of taking a profit on any single trade in the securities markets. With two commissions, a state tax, and a Securities Exchange Commission (SEC) fee to pay, the customer would not seem to be the favorite.

several ways to do this. I will point them out, but it's you who must observe the precautions. I have never forgotten the story of the young man who took his mother's life savings (without her knowledge or consent) and bet them on Native Dancer to win the Kentucky Derby of 1953. Native Dancer had won everything in sight up to that time and went off a 7 to 10 favorite. He lost by a neck, the only time he failed to finish first in his entire racing career. Twenty-one wins out of twenty-two starts isn't bad, but which race do you think the young man and his mother remember?

I will show you how to prevent big losses, but you must cooperate by not exposing yourself to excessive risks. It's not good for the metabolism, and it's unnecessary. I will communicate everything I know, describe all of the methods, techniques, and rules I follow in consistently taking profits. I will explain in detail what I consider a practical and profitable approach for the small investor. But it is imperative that you do not go for the quick killing, the one trade that will set you up on Easy Street. Anybody who tries this is automatically exposing himself to too much risk. And such risk is diametrically opposed in spirit and in principle to what I recommend. The approach I've taken involves accumulating sensible profits steadily and consistently with minimal risk. The objective is to build substantial capital over a period of time, not to try to make it quickly by hazarding everything on one or two transactions.

One last caution: some people may be temperamentally unsuited to making the decisions my method of trading requires. If you find yourself losing sleep, snapping at your family, or kicking the cat, it may be that options trading is not your game.

If you do enter the listed options marketplaces and you protect yourself from loss as suggested, and use the profit strategies which have worked so consistently for me, large profits are feasible. If you add to large percentage gains on each investment the effect of compounding consistent profits, the opportunity for amassing serious sums of money is clear.

2. Deliverance

Because my first book, *How I Turn Ordinary Complaints Into Thousands of Dollars: The Diary of a Tough Customer,* had been a best seller, there were some who thought I'd made at least a million dollars and was living off the income. The truth was that, having resigned from my job at one of the television networks, I had eventually spent more than the book had netted and was living out of capital.

I had set up a corporation to deal in films, television programs, books, and other media rights. We had been nibbling through our life's savings for more than a year and were running out of cash, but we'd managed to put about $8,000 into our corporate pension and profit-sharing accounts. This was money that could be invested but not spent by us until we were 59½, without incurring prohibitive taxes and penalties.

As there are ordinarily no taxes to be paid on any increments in these retirement accounts, most people are inclined to invest the funds fairly conservatively. A return of 8 or 10 percent or so, tax free, is considered not bad, and it keeps compounding over the years. But most people of this conservative bent have a job or other steady source of income; we didn't. When you're using up your life's savings at the rate we were, 8 or 10 percent is not attractive. I thought I could do twice as well as that. After all, before joining the network, I'd spent nine years in the so-called financial community and had run a Wall Street securities business that bore my name.

A typical objective of many money managers is 15 percent, for which they get pretty good fees and other benefits whether or not that objective is achieved, which it often isn't. I decided to pay for some advice and plunked down $150 for a three-month trial subscription to an investment advisory service, the work of the man whose opinion on the market I most respected, Edson Gould.

Gould has had a long and distinguished career. Among other accomplishments, he has called market tops and bottoms with uncanny precision for decades. A three-month subscription for $150 is a pretty good number, but I thought Edson and I could provide us with better than a 15 percent tax-free yield, and I was willing to pay to find out.

My first two stock trades, following Gould's advice, netted a grand total of $77.53. The commissions, state taxes, and SEC fees amounted to a somewhat disproportionate $197.47, not to mention the $150 for the trial subscription.

In the thirty-one-page report dated November 21, 1974, Gould recommended The Upjohn Company in an eight-page section. The company was strong, the stock had sold for more than $100 per share in 1973 and had been higher than $88 in 1974. I bought 100 shares at 46½.

After the order to buy Upjohn was placed, my customers' broker told me there were listed options on Upjohn, which were traded on the Chicago Board Options Exchange. I had done a few trades in *un*listed options over the years and had made and lost money, mostly lost. But *listed* options were something new. I began to ask question and, as the broker responded, dazzling possibilities for making money flooded my mind. Next day, the Options Clearing Corporation prospectus arrived, sent by the broker, and I spent the morning studying it in detail. It was now clear to me that I had been right. There really were exciting new ways to take profits that didn't exist in all the years I'd worked on Wall Street. Because of a chance remark from a customers' broker I had stumbled through the looking glass and was now beginning to explore profit possibilities on the other side.

During the next three weeks, I took my first two profits in listed options, more than $1,000! I still read Mr. Gould's reports the same day they arrived, but not with the same eagerness. The two consecutive profits were welcome, but I wanted to develop a systematic approach to winning consistently at this new game. I was reasonably sure it could be done. Between Christmas and the beginning of the New Year I stayed home, working on the problem. Frankly, I didn't feel much like attending social functions. It was getting harder and harder to take people who used the word "lifestyle" too much and chattered about "in" places and "out" islands while my checkbooks were down to about the same numbers as the lunch and dinner tabs I'd been signing.

By the end of the seventh business day of 1975, I had taken five additional profits. I knew I was on to something exciting in listed options and thought a book would be the ideal format for presenting it. The publisher of my first book was interested and we scheduled a meeting for February 3.

By that date, I'd run the score to twenty-one consecutive profits! The publisher and I tried to decide on an impressive number of consecutive profits that would be feasible within a limited period of time. I came up with the number fifty-one; the publisher thought forty-six in six months would be convincing.

I found charming the idea of two adults blithely discussing over lunch what might be a world record, if accomplished. I also was much taken by the fact that the publisher was taking me at my word in an area in which he wasn't very knowledgeable. He was ready to make a commitment and lay out some money up front; he hadn't asked me to come back later, *after* I'd done it.

Once we agreed on the terms of the contract, the pressure was on. The little old lady from Pasadena *may* step up to a dice table in Las Vegas and throw forty-six passes in a row without a single loss, but she hasn't signed a contract in advance to do so. I knew that if I failed the egg on my face wouldn't feed the family, and that I might also have to return the advance payment on the book long after it had been spent. Nevertheless, I was aiming for the fifty-one profits I had originally suggested.

On April 23, 1975, less than five months from the November 26 start date, I had forty-five consecutive profits in the pension and the profit-sharing accounts, plus six consecutive profits in a small account in the names of my wife and myself—a total of fifty-one consecutive profits without a single loss. Now that the contractual obligation had been kept, I wanted to be able to trade the three accounts in a way that would produce the biggest gains, even if that meant occasionally taking a loss so as not to have cash tied up too long in an unprofitable trade. It may sound odd but it is actually easier to make more money, particularly with a small investment, if an occasional loss is taken. The stricture of working against an arbitrary deadline and therefore always having to take profits quickly also limited the total dollar amount of profits taken. Having to separate a relatively small sum into three different accounts made trading unwieldy, increased the commissions, and was thus another limiting factor. There were times when there were insufficient amounts of money available in any one of the accounts which, if lumped together, would have been sufficient to make a trade. Also, four options, bought or sold as a single order, are much less expensive to trade than two options bought or sold in one account and a single option bought or sold in each of two other accounts.

These limitations, in the aggregate, sharply reduced my total profits. And even if it made sense to get out of something at a small loss so that I could immediately put the money into a potentially profitable situation, I couldn't do so because of that one stricture: no losses. Like an Olympic runner, I had to abide by very tough training rules.

I also made mistakes at the beginning that wasted not money, but time, because I was perfecting the method as I went along. With all of these limitations, the forty-five consecutive profits totaled $6,806.68 in less than five months on an initial $8,000.00 investment. This is a rate of profit of 13.1 percent *compounded monthly,* an annualized gain of 338 percent, more than 22½ times the typical 15 percent money managers try to achieve. At that rate, my $8,000.00 would become $2,946,419.70 in four years. And if I wanted to trade options full time, I would certainly buy a seat on one of the exchanges. The commissions that would have been saved would have amounted to $3,419.28 on the forty-five profits.

The six consecutive profits in the other small account

netted more than 61 percent in two and one-half months, an extraordinary 21 percent gain, *compounded monthly,* an 885 percent annual gain. Although I had to take profits only and had only a tiny sum to work with, I had the benefit of all of the methods set forth in this book and had learned from my previous errors. The 885 percent annual rate at which this account grew is fifty-nine times the 15 percent objective typical of money managers.

What I think makes this book worth reading is this combination of factors:

1. I did it. The book is based on the author's actual firsthand experience, not on vague theory.

2. In doing it, I used only my own and my wife's money. This is not the case history of some money manager who has selected the one special success story from among hundreds of accounts that fared less well.

3. What I did can be duplicated. There is a method involved. In developing the method, I made some early mistakes, which will be pointed out so that you can avoid them. Although these mistakes did not cause any losses, they did waste time. Had I known at the outset what I know now, the results would have been even better.

The method is fully explained in these pages. I have held nothing back. Because hundreds of dollars worth of listed options can control several thousands of dollars worth of stock, only a relatively modest sum is needed. This permits the small investor to enjoy this new profit potential. I am convinced that, using my system, the small investor can turn steady, worthwhile profits within acceptable limits of risk. But if a lot of money isn't necessary, a certain amount of time and effort *are* required if the methods and techniques of this new game are to be mastered. Most readers will probably be entering a strange, new world and they will have to move slowly and cautiously at first. Only those willing to learn this new game well and to continue to give the time necessary to play it intelligently may rightfully expect to reap its rewards.

3. The Way We Were

Do you remember those medical series on prime-time television that opened with a massive effort to save the life of an emergency patient? I don't mean kindly old doctor shows like *Marcus Welby;* he's in private practice. I mean the ones where the star is a doctor in a hospital, like *Ben Casey.* With appropriately "heroic" music under the action, we are given quick cuts of orchestrated teamwork enlisted in the fight for life against death. The patient is finally placed aboard an ambulance and, with sound effects and music rising to a crescendo, raced to the hospital emergency entrance. More white-clad team members are there to rush the victim down corridors toward the emergency room—and life—while the music really comes into its own.

Well, if you add a couple of bottles of intravenous solution, a pulmotor and an iron lung (and take away the music) and then have the ambulance totaled by a befuddled Sunday driver, the metaphor would be about right for that poor creature who's been carried out more times than the garbage—the small investor. Talk about deep sixing. The small investor has been buried so many times he can no longer see in the light.

However, a scant 181 years after the founding of the

New York Stock Exchange under the famed buttonwood tree on Wall Street, something startlingly new and different was added to the old "own your share of American business" medicine show. At long last, it became possible for the small investor, who had been clobbered so regularly, to consistently come out ahead. I refer, of course, to the Chicago Board Options Exchange (C.B.O.E.), which commenced trading operations on April 26, 1973. On that historic date the public was offered a package of new opportunities to make substantial gains. The extraordinary and unprecedented profit potentials which the C.B.O.E. made available to everybody are truly revolutionary.

But before discussing the new ways to make money with listed options we should be clear as to what an option—any option—is. The option contract has been a well-recognized way of doing business for centuries. References to options may be found in the Old Testament and in ancient Greek, Phoenician, and Roman writings. Options contracts, in ordinary commercial dealings, allow the option buyer to control a relatively large amount of property for a relatively small sum, providing leverage and limited total risk. At the same time, the option seller (or writer)* received money (the premium) for contracting to make available the property optioned at a stated price (the exercise price or striking price) within a specified period of time (until the expiration date of the option).

Let us assume, for example, that you come across some real or personal property that can be purchased for $100,000. You are aware that a buyer can be interested in this property at a price of $110,000. You may not have, or do not wish to tie up, $100,000 in this way. If you did buy

* All of the technical terms used in this book are defined in the glossary.

the property for $100,000 you might find that the prospective buyer had changed his mind. Similarly, if you contracted to sell the property for $110,000 before making sure you could buy it at a lower price, you might find it unavailable. Furthermore, if you approached the prospective buyer without having your right to acquire the property secured, nothing could prevent the prospective buyer from dealing directly with the owner.

If, however, you could buy an option on the property for a small sum of money (perhaps a few hundred dollars) which would give you the right to buy it for a relatively short period of time at a price of $100,000, you would have an opportunity to enter into a contract with the prospective buyer at a price of $110,000 without risking a large sum. If you were successful, you would realize a substantial percentage gain on the amount you risked—that is, the few hundred dollars spent on the option.

Let's look at one more example of this kind of option before we discuss options on stocks. Suppose an independent movie producer reads or sees a play that he * would like to produce as a film. If he bought the film rights he might find he was unable to raise the money with which to make the movie. In that case he would have a fairly substantial amount of money tied up in the property and he might not be able to sell what he'd bought at a profit or, indeed, at any price.

If the producer could buy an option on the play which would give him enough time to try to put a package together (script, stars, director) and interest a distributor or other source of money, he would reduce his initial risk

---

* All masculine nouns and pronouns are intended to include the feminine as well as masculine gender, unless otherwise indicated.

considerably and still have the opportunity to make the picture. Again, the option would give him high leverage (the ability to control the rights to the play for a relatively small sum) and limited total risk (if he chose not to exercise the option and could not sell it at any price, he would lose only the premium—that is, the relatively small price he paid for the option).

Options contracts contain certain essential elements:

1. a complete description of what is being optioned

2. the price to be paid if the option is exercised (the exercise price or the striking price)

3. a time limit: a point in time at which the option expires.

While not a term of the option contract, the premium is the sum of money paid for the option to the seller of the option; this sum is kept by the seller whether or not the option is exercised.

Let's now look at options on stock. A call option, or simply a call, is an option to buy designated property at a stated price by a certain date. Both options discussed so far—the one involving the property that could be bought for $100,000 and the one involving the play—are examples of call options. All of the profits I took and all of the profit strategies in this book involve call options. Furthermore, during the early years of listed options trading, the call option was the only type of option traded on any of the exchanges.

Each call option on stock involves 100 shares of stock. If, for example, you want to buy call options on 500 shares of a particular stock, you buy five calls (not one call on 500 shares).

Let's now look at what calls were like prior to April 26,

1973, the date the Chicago Board Options Exchange made listed options available for the first time and thus introduced a number of profit-extending and loss-limiting capabilities.

Before the organization of the C.B.O.E., options were normally bought and sold through put and call brokers and dealers. You may have seen advertisements in *The Wall Street Journal* and other financial publications that looked like this:

XYZ Options Co.

CALLS

77⅛	ASA Ltd.	70¾	3 mos.	1000.00
27¾	Fairchild Camera	26¾	Apr. 14	375.00
91¼	Johnson & Johnson	84½	6 mos.	1175.00
34	Marath. Oil	33¾	May 13	387.50
15½	Scott Paper	13	May 13	362.50

subject to prior sale or price change

XYZ Options Co.
185 Wall St. N.Y., N.Y.
Tel. 212 052 1790
Members Put and Call
Brokers & Dealers Assoc.

The number to the left of the name of the stock refers to its closing price the day prior to the appearance of the ad. The number to the right of the stock's name is the exercise price or striking price. This is followed by the expiration date and the premium. Anybody who wished to enter into any of the options contracts advertised would not deal directly with the put and call broker but through a brokerage firm which was a member of a national exchange, like the New York Stock Exchange, for example. The member firm would guarantee the options contract.

The Fairchild Camera call, for example, would have given the buyer the right to buy 100 shares of Fairchild Camera common stock at a price of $26.75 per share (or $2,675 ° for 100 shares) at any time until April 14, 1975, for which the option buyer would have paid a premium of $375.

The buyer of this Fairchild Camera call might have had a number of motives for so doing, but basically he is attracted by two considerations: leverage and limited total risk. If, between the date he buys this call and April 14, 1975, Fairchild Camera rose fourteen points, that is, from 27¾ (the closing price shown at the left of the name of the stock) to a price of 41¾ per share, the buyer of 100 shares at 27¾ would have gained $1,400 (gross; see previous foot-note) about 50 percent on his investment. The buyer of the call would have grossed $1,500 (he could sell the stock at 41¾ and call it at 26¾) minus the premium of $375, or a gain of about 300 percent on an original investment of $375. The option would have yielded more than six times the percentage gain as the stock purchased for cash. This is an example of leverage at work.

And much less money would have been at risk. Fairchild Camera common stock might have declined to a price of $10 per share, subjecting the buyer of the stock to a real or paper loss of $1,775, whereas the buyer of the call would

° Commissions, taxes, and fees are omitted to simplify the arithmetic in this section of the book; when my actual trades are discussed, all charges are taken into consideration.

stand to lose no more than the $375 he paid for the option, no matter how far down the stock went. In addition, if he'd wanted to he could have put the difference between the price of the stock and the price of the call ($2,400) into another investment or into the bank at interest. This exemplifies the idea of limited total risk.

Advertisements like the one illustrated are placed by put and call brokers and dealers. The offerings listed are a few of their "special options." These are options they have in inventory. They are available in limited quantities and are offered subject to prior sale or price change. An individual interested in any of these special options would typically ask his customers' broker to shop the street, that is, ask other put and call brokers and dealers for terms on options on Fairchild Camera. In selling a special option out of his own inventory, the put and call company is acting in its capacity as a dealer, or principal. It also acts as a broker (an agent) when it is the middleman who arranges the purchase or sale of options between a buyer and a seller.

We have seen what motivates the buyer of an unlisted option. For every purchase there must be a sale of an equal amount at the same price. What motivates the seller to create the option? The typical seller of such an option probably holds Fairchild Camera for the long term. He expects the price of the stock to rise over the course of time but not to do so quickly. He wants to gain the premium. He is willing, if necessary, to sell 100 shares of the stock at the exercise price plus the premium (in this case $2,675 plus $375). And he doesn't expect the stock to drop drastically in price before the call expires. The seller is, in effect, betting that the stock doesn't go way down in price during the life of the call (and thinks it won't go way up either, but he is less concerned about this). Should the stock remain stationary in price or move up or down slightly, he is satisfied to gain all—or most—of the premium for holding it. And if the stock goes up sharply, he is willing to accept the exercise price of the stock plus the premium. Should the stock remain at about 27¾ he will net the premium of $375, as the call would not be exercised. Should the stock decline he would be protected against loss on the downside to the extent of the premium.

Most unlisted options, other than special options, are bought and sold "at the market" (the striking price or exercise price is the same as the previous price at which the stock sold when the option contract is entered into). However, contracts "away from the market" may be negotiated. That is, the exercise price may be above or below the previous price (last sale) at which the stock traded. The Fairchild Camera option was "away from the market" as the exercise price (26¾) was not the same as the last sale (27¾). The terms involved in unlisted option contracts (expiration date, striking price) as well as the premium or price of the option, are negotiable. These negotiations usually involve telephone conversations between the put and call broker/dealer and the buyer's and seller's broker.

As it is the purpose of this book to describe profitable opportunities in the new, *listed* options, I have tried to keep this introductory discussion of unlisted options brief and untechnical. It is therefore necessarily incomplete. Unlisted options can and do serve a useful function and much has been written on the subject. Anybody interested might ask a customers' broker to supply further information. Put and call broker/dealers and/or their association may also be able to furnish printed material.

Now that the basic facts about options in general and unlisted options have been presented, we are ready to look into the exciting new realm of listed options.

4. The Making of a Precedent

Despite deepening gloom on Wall Street and a precipitous decline that shredded share prices from the inception of the Chicago Board Options Exchange until the end of 1974,* the C.B.O.E. enjoyed outstanding success by every measurement. At first, options on only sixteen stocks were available. This number has since risen to seventy-nine. In addition, there has been an increase in the number of different exercise prices and expiration dates of each individual stock, further expanding the opportunities for profit. In May 1973, the first full month of trading, daily volume on the C.B.O.E. averaged 1,600 contracts. In January 1975, daily volume averaged more than 42,000 contracts, involving more than 4,200,000 shares of stock. By this measurement, the C.B.O.E. became second in the nation to the New York Stock Exchange. Daily volume has exceeded 100,000 contracts on several occasions, representing more than ten million shares.

The C.B.O.E. handled more than 5,600,000 contracts in 1974, and the dollar volume of trading exceeded $200

* Total value of stocks traded on the New York Stock Exchange declined an estimated 27%, or approximately $196.5 billion, in 1974 alone.

million,* and was rising. Open interest (the number of outstanding contracts) increased from an average of 99,000 during the period from April through December 1973 to 330,000 from January to October 1974. Open interest has risen further in 1975 and 1976.

On January 13, 1975 the American Stock Exchange (Amex) began to trade in options. On that date options or only two striking prices and two expiration dates were available on six underlying stocks. Nevertheless, the opening day's volume of 1,868 contracts was more than double the 911 traded on the opening day of the C.B.O.E. A week later Amex options on twenty stocks were available, and with many additional striking prices and expiration dates. Before the end of 1975 there were Amex options on forty stocks and the American Stock Exchange had applied to the Securities and Exchange Commission for permission to expand the list by twenty stocks.

A seat on the C.B.O.E. was originally offered at $10,000 and sold for as much as $75,000 in a little more than two years. From a yearly low of $27,000 on April 18, 1974, the price of an Amex seat rose to $72,000 on December 18, 1974, exactly what had been paid for a seat on the New York Stock Exchange twenty-two days earlier. This was the first time in history that the last sale price of an Amex seat and a seat on the New York Stock Exchange were equal. The reason was clear: options were soon to be traded on the Amex and volume was certain to rise.

The public acceptance of listed options influenced another exchange, the PBW (formerly Philadelphia-Baltimore-Washington), to begin trading. Ten stocks already

---

* In premiums paid, not in the dollar value of the underlying stocks, which was in the neighborhood of $2 billion.

have listed options trading on the PBW, with more to come. The Pacific Stock Exchange is expected to follow shortly. In Canada, the Montreal Stock Exchange has already begun trading options and the Toronto and Vancouver exchanges also hope to begin trading options soon. A European options exchange is a possibility in London or Amsterdam, and exchanges in Manila, Singapore, Sydney, Japan, and Rio de Janeiro are planning to trade options soon. On September 15, 1975, the board of the National Association of Securities Dealers endorsed the concept of a standardized market for trading options in over-the-counter securities. Even the New York Stock Exhcange is looking into the possibility of trading options.

By the end of 1975, listed call options were being bought and sold on the following stocks:

Chicago Board Options Exchange

A E P	Citicorp
A M P	Commonwealth Edison
Alcoa	Coke
Amerada Hess	Colgate
American Telephone	Delta
Atlantic Richfield	Dow Chemical
Avon Products	Eastman Kodak
Baxter Labs.	Exxon
Bethlehem Steel	F N M
Black & Decker	Ford
Boeing	General Motors
Brunswick	General Electric
C B S	General Foods
Control Data	Gulf & Western

General Dynamics
Great Western
   Financial
Holiday Inns
Haliburton
Hewlett-Packard
Homestake Mining
Honeywell
I B M
I N A
I T T
Int'l Flavors
Int'l Harvester
Int'l Minerals
Int'l Paper
Johns-Manville
Jim Walter
Johnson & Johnson
Kennecott Copper
Kerr-McGee
Kresge
Loews
M M M
McDonnell
Merck
Mobil

Monsanto
Nat'l Semiconductor
Northwest Airlines
Occidental Petroleum
Pennzoil
Polaroid
R C A
Raytheon
Reynolds (R.J.)
Sears
Skyline.
Schlumberger
Southern Co.
Sperry
Standard Oil of Indiana
Syntex
Tesoro
Texas Instruments
Texas Gulf
U A L
United Tech.
Upjohn
Utah Int'l
Weyerhaeuser
Williams Co.
Xerox

Amex Options

A M F
A S A
Aetna

American Cyanimid
American Home Products
Beatrice Foods

Amex Options (continued)

Burroughs	Motorola
Caterpillar Tractor	Pfizer
Chase Manhattan	Philip Morris
Deere	Phelps Dodge
Digital Equipment	Phillips Petroleum
Disney	Procter & Gamble
du Pont	Searle
First Charter Financial	Standard Oil of California
General Telephone	Sterling Drug
Gillette	Tenneco
Goodyear	Texaco
Grace	Tiger Int'l
Greyhound	Union Carbide
Gulf Oil	U.S. Steel
Hercules	Westinghouse
Merrill Lynch	Warner-Lambert
Mesa Petroleum	Zenith

PBW Options

Abbott Laboratories
Allied Chemical
Boise Cascade
Continental Oil
Engelhard
Firestone
Howard Johnson
Louisiana Land
Virginia Electric Power
Woolworth

These are not the kinds of cats and dogs to be picked up at the local ASPCA. All of these common stocks are widely held and actively traded. And among the names on these rosters are many of the bluest blue-chip American corporate equities.

All of the exchanges on which options are listed and traded are registered national securities exchanges. The exchanges and their members are subject to the Securities Exchange Act of 1934 and the regulatory jurisdiction of the Securities and Exchange Commission. And the options themselves are registered securities under the Securities Act of 1933.

I believe the introduction of listed options has been such a success because they offer new and unique opportunities for profit for both buyers and sellers, particularly when their purchase or sale is coupled with other action, as described and illustrated in these pages. We will examine exactly how impressive profits may be derived from listed options in the next chapter. First, however, we should begin to become familiar with the fundamentals of the listed options game.

One of the primary results of listed options trading is to provide a new marketplace in which options may be traded, in very much the way listed warrants are currently traded. A warrant, like a call option, is an option to buy the stock underlying it at a stated price for a specific length of time. The key difference between a warrant and a call option is the manner by which each comes into being. Warrants are created by the corporation that creates the underlying stock, usually as a way of making a new securities offering of the corporation more attractive to a potential purchaser. Listed call options may be created by anybody who cares to sell one and is willing to follow the rules of the exchange on which it trades and those of the member firm or other brokerage house with which he deals.

The exchanges, in addition to providing a marketplace for the buying and selling of listed options and safeguarding them with a number of protections, have standardized the options themselves with respect to striking prices and expiration dates. Only the premiums remain unfixed in advance and they are subject to bids and offers on the same basis of supply and demand as any other listed security.

Let us look at an example which should explain the concept of listed options and distinguish listed from unlisted options. You might see a listing in a financial publication that looks like this: °

CHICAGO BOARD OPTIONS EXCHANGE
March 4, 1975

	April		July		Oct.		Stock
	Vol.	Last	Vol.	Last	Vol.	Last	Close
Kennecott Copper35	246	2⅝	200	4⅛	47	4⅞	35⅝
Kennecott Copper40	269	⅞	92	2¼	35	2⅞	35⅝

"Kennecott Copper35" means that the striking price or exercise price of this option is $35 per share. As all listed options on the date of this listing (March 4, 1975) were call options, it was not necessary to specify that it, too, was a call. We have already seen that all listed options involve 100 shares of the underlying stock; in this case, the underlying stock is Kennecott Copper. One Kennecott Copper35 call option would permit its owner to purchase

° *The Wall Street Journal* uses this format, which I consider the clearest presentation of the data, particularly for beginners.

100 shares of Kennecott Copper common stock at a price of $35 per share, or $3,500 (plus a commission) until it expired. "April," "July," and "Oct." refer to the expiration months of the options. The April options will expire toward the end of April, etc. Beginning with January, 1976 C.B.O.E. options, buyers will have until the third Saturday of the expiration month to *exercise* calls and until the third Friday of the expiration month to *sell* calls. Sellers will also have until the third Friday of the expiration month to *buy* calls. This is the rule of the Chicago Board Options Exchange with respect to last trading day and last day to exercise options. These rules may vary from exchange to exchange. In addition, brokerage houses may require earlier notice so they can clear up their paper work. At this point it is sufficient to know that there is a specific date beyond which a particular call may not be bought, sold, or exercised.

The figures in the column headed "Vol." refer to the volume of trading: that is, the number of calls traded on the date shown (March 4, 1975). The Kennecott Copper April35 traded 246 calls. This means that the number bought or sold on that date was 246. It takes one buyer of a call and one seller of a call to create a trading volume of one.

The column headed "Last" refers to the closing price or last sale price of the option that day. The Kennecott Copper April35, for example, closed at 2⅝. This price, or premium, must be multiplied by 100 to determine how much the option buyer paid for an option on 100 shares—$262.50.

The column at the extreme right, "Stock Close," refers to the last sale or closing price of the stock (not the option)—Kennecott Copper common stock, in this case.

Kennecott Copper common stock closed at 35⅝, or $35.62½ per share, on March 4, 1975.

The only difference between the Kennecott Copper April35 and the Kennecott Copper July35 (apart from their prices or premiums) is the fact that the July option has three months more time in which to trade before it expires. It is this additional trading life that makes the July option more valuable than the April; it includes possibilities for both buyers and sellers that the April option does not have. The value of this additional trading life is reflected in the fact that the Kennecott Copper April35 traded last at a price of 2⅝ while the Kennecott Copper July35 traded last at 4⅛ on the date shown. These price differentials are sometimes greater, sometimes less than might be expected in relation to the time left until expiration. We will examine this aspect more closely when we look at the various ways to profit.

Similarly, the only difference between the Kennecott April35 and the Kennecott April40 (apart from their premiums) is the fact that their striking prices are five points (five dollars per share) apart. An option that gives the buyer the right to buy the underlying stock for five dollars less for the same length of time is obviously more valuable. In this case, the Kennecott Copper April35 closed at 2⅝ while the Kennecott Copper April40 closed at ⅞, a difference of 1¾. I have seen cases in which options on the same underlying stock, same expiration date, and a five-point difference in striking prices trade at differences of a small fraction of a dollar to a full five points and even slightly more. Whether the market appears to be undervaluing or overvaluing this difference will provide opportunities for profit, as we will see later.

Listed options meet the requirements of liquidity, flexibility, and market efficiency that unlisted options lack. Buyers and sellers of listed options may follow their prices or premiums precisely as they follow the price fluctuations of a listed stock. There is a separate tape on which options transactions appear. In addition, prices of listed options have been incorporated into all of the major quoting systems and are also reported in the financial press. Buyers and sellers of listed options are able to reverse their positions at will. It is by virtue of these new features in the options markets that attractive profit opportunities on a regular basis and with reduced risks are now available.

A little more background may be helpful before we get to the various profit strategies.

The Options Clearing Corporation is a joint clearing company that is involved as a principal in the settlement of options transactions on the C.B.O.E., Amex, and PBW exchanges. Therefore, unlike the way unlisted options function, it is no longer necessary to be obligated to the person with whom you originally made your options contracts. Buyers and sellers are no longer tied to one another: both have obligations to the Options Clearing Corporation. This frees both buyers and sellers to reverse their positions at will. The writer or seller of a listed option is no longer bound by the commitment to make available the stock on which he sold the option, at a stated price (the exercise price) until the option expires. He now has the further choice of reversing his trade in the marketplace any time he wants to do so prior to being asked to deliver the stock on which the option was written. (We will examine the alternatives available to a writer, or seller, of listed options if he is called for delivery of the stock when we discuss the many ways to profit, beginning in the next chapter.) Reversing his position simply means buying an option in the marketplace which has the same exercise price and the same expiration date on the same stock as the one he sold and asking his customers' broker to match the option bought with the option sold.

The Options Clearing Corporation will then cancel his position on their books. The difference between what he received for the option he sold and what he paid for the option he bought (including commissions) will determine the extent of his profit or loss. In exactly the same way, the buyer of a listed option may later sell the option he bought in the marketplace. These offsetting trades are called closing transactions. In the case of a listed option buyer, of course, there is no chance of his being asked to deliver stock since this obligation applies only to sellers.

Options trading on the C.B.O.E., the Amex, and the PBW options exchanges are similar in most respects. The minor differences in some of the procedures on the various listed options exchanges need not concern us at this point, as they do not affect our basic approaches to profits.

There are two kinds of margin requirements: the percentage of the total purchase price required to put on or position a new commitment in your account is called "original margin"; the money needed to hold your position if the market goes against you is called "maintenance margin." These margin requirements, as well as commission rates and house rules, vary from firm to firm and from time to time. Prior to May 1, 1975, the minimum commissions on the C.B.O.E. were as follows:

On orders for the purchase or sale of a single option—

Money Involved in the Order	Minimum Commission
less than $100	as mutually agreed
$100-2,499	1.3% plus $12 (minimum $25)
2,500-4,777	0.9% plus $22
4,778-30,000	$65

On orders for the purchase or sale of more than one option:

Money Involved in the Order	Minimum Commission
less than $100	as mutually agreed (we paid 8.4%)
$100-2,499	1.3% plus $12
2,500-19,999	0.9% plus $22
20,000-30,000	0.6% plus $82
more than $30,000	subject to negotiation

plus $6 per option for the *first* to tenth option covered by the order; $4 per option for each additional option covered by the order.

On May 1, 1975, the minimum commissions schedules were abolished and commissions became "negotiable." The commissions you will be charged may be obtained from a broker on request.

It is important to become familiar with the rules that apply before entering into any transactions. Slight savings on commissions may not necessarily yield the best net results, as there are other variables, such as quality of handling customer orders, accessibility to your customers' broker, his expertise and attitude and that of the brokerage house, that may be more important.

The hours of trading on the listed options exchanges are the same as the trading hours on the New York Stock Exchange, 10 A.M. to 4 P.M. Eastern time. Very low-priced options are traded in minimum variations of 1/16 of a dollar. Above a certain minimum (either two dollars or three dollars on the various exchanges, but this is subject to change), the minimum variation is 1/8 of a dollar. Unlike unlisted options, listed options are not adjusted to reflect ordinary cash dividends. Unlisted options have their exercise prices lowered to reflect the payment of cash dividends; listed options maintain their original exercise prices regardless of cash dividends. Of course, if a stock splits or pays a stock dividend, the exercise price will be changed to reflect such changes.

A particular stock may have listed options of several different striking prices. These striking prices are set in relation to the price of the stock at the time the new option month begins to trade. Current practice is to add striking prices in five-point intervals in options in which the stocks are selling under $50 per share; in ten-point intervals for stocks between $50 and $200 per share, and in twenty-point intervals for stocks above $200 per share. Additional higher or lower striking prices are added in these intervals to reflect price changes in the stock. For example, in the Kennecott Copper illustration on page 36, should the price of Kennecott Copper fall to 32½ (the mid-point of the interval), a Kennecott Copper30 would become eligible for trading and would join the Kennecott Copper35 and the

Kennecott Copper40, as striking prices may not be removed until all option months trading a particular striking price have expired. These additional striking prices, as we will see, often multiply the opportunities for profit.

In the next chapter we will begin to examine the many ways of obtaining profits through the use of listed options. Before going further, however, please note a few words of caution:

This introductory material is not meant to be exhaustive. In the interest of brevity, some points may have been given improper weight. Many of the procedural rules have been abbreviated. Interested readers should become better acquainted with the rules, some of which may well have changed by the time this book is published. The Options Clearing Corporation prospectus would be the ideal starting point for learning the rules. This prospectus is widely available, and any firm trading in options and any exchange trading them can make a copy available to you at no cost.

There are many rules and by-laws governing listed options exchanges; there are also federal regulations and each firm has its own house rules. Knowledge of the rules is certainly advised before entering any game. Some of the current rules are summarized in the relevant sections but there is no way to cover them all in a book of this size.

On the title page of the Options Clearing Corporation prospectus there is a paragraph in bold-faced type to the effect that buying and selling options involves a high degree of risk and that options are not suitable for many investors. The same paragraph cautions that options transactions should be entered into only by investors who have read and understood the prospectus and who understand the nature and extent of their rights and obligations and are aware of the risks involved. Investors are further cautioned not to buy options unless they are able to sustain a loss of their entire investment. And they are advised not to sell, or write, an option unless they either own the underlying security or are able to sustain substantial financial losses.

Without in any way gainsaying these cautions, I believe that by following my approach the careful investor can reduce these risks considerably. I have taken dozens of consecutive profits without a single loss in the listed options market, whereas previously in the stock market I showed losses as well as profits. Some of the most sophisticated money managers are using options to improve their performance records, and many conservative investors are also discovering options. I would readily concede that listed options are not for everybody. Whether or not they are for you is a highly subjective decision.

The next chapter contains an enormous amount of concentrated material. Anybody unfamiliar with the subject matter should not be discouraged if he finds it somewhat hard to grasp the first time. This book is meant to be a course in making money by means of listed options. It cannot be read and understood at the same speed as a novel. Even the rules of Monopoly were difficult to understand at first. But after you played the game a few times, it all seemed very simple. This book requires more of the reader than the rules of Monopoly, but I think the analogy is sound. I can promise that if you give it some time and study and practice it will get easier and easier. And when you're ready, if you decide to play, I hope you will share in both the profits and the fun of the listed options game.

5. Profit Strategies

In making a decision as to whether or not to commit funds to a specific profit opportunity, I try to evaluate three elements: profit potential, risk, and cost. (I am also aware that a fourth element—taxes—may play a part in both the commitment and its liquidation.) If the mix is sufficiently attractive, I buy it; if not, I wait for a better opportunity.

RISK CONSIDERATIONS

It may seem paradoxical that my primary consideration involves evaluation of risk. Many people think of a trader as some kind of wild gambler who bets his roll on the turn of a card. As a trader in options, preservation of capital is my paramount consideration. Toward that end I look for a high degree of certainty of gain, rather than all or nothing at all. It seems prudent to gain steadily rather than to try to gain big or lose big. The steady compounding of even small profits yields extremely attractive gains. Winning big and losing big puts a strain not only on financial resources but on emotional resources as well.

The questions we will be addressing in the risk area are:

What is the most I can lose? How likely am I to lose the maximum? How likely is any loss?

PROFIT CONSIDERATIONS

The questions here are fairly clear: What is the *most* I can gain? How likely am I to gain close to the maximum? How likely is *any* gain?

COST CONSIDERATIONS

How much do I have to put up to make the particular commitment being considered? Do I need any cash reserves beyond that? Is the profit potential sufficiently attractive to commit these funds?

TAX CONSIDERATIONS

If I gain, how do I legally keep the most net dollars? If I lose, how do I legally minimize the net loss?

We will be looking at all of these factors. However, in order to facilitate the presentation of a great deal of concentrated material that may not be familiar to many readers, and because tax considerations are not of the same importance to me as the other factors and would not be to most readers, tax consequences are treated separately later.

In organizing the material I have tried to keep each of the basic strategies as brief and uncluttered as possible. In the material entitled "Extra Points" and in the section describing my own trading there are additional suggestions that may be useful in sharpening your play. It is not absolutely necessary to master all of the strategies in order to profit from any one of them. The plays are all separate and may be used independently. However, at a minimum, I would advise a complete and thorough reading of this book and the Options Clearing Corporation prospectus, a familiarity with the rules and procedures which would apply under actual playing conditions, and satisfactory practice on paper before actually trading a single option.

6. Spreads

How would you like to make a commitment in which for every $100 you invest your maximum loss was predetermined and could not exceed about $100; your maximum gain would approach $500, and the chances of profit were excellent? If you would, then spreads is your game, for this and a bundle of other profit opportunities are available with spreads.

A spread may be defined as a position in which one or more calls involving the same underlying stock are both bought and sold, and in which the calls bought differ in striking price or expiration date, or both, from the calls sold. The following are all examples of spreads:

Bought 1 Polaroid July25 at 2¾
Sold 3 Polaroid April25 at 1¾

In this example, the underlying stock on both the buy and the sell side is Polaroid common stock. The position involves one or more calls bought and one or more calls sold, and the expiration dates are different (July and April).

Bought 2 Polaroid July20 at 4¾
Sold 2 Polaroid July25 at 2¾

Again, the underlying stock is the same on both the buy and sell sides; one or more calls have been bought and sold, and the striking prices are different (20 and 25). Note that a spread may involve buying and selling an equal or unequal number of calls.

Bought 5 Polaroid July20 at 4¾
Sold 8 Polaroid April25 at 1¾

In this case, the underlying stock on both sides is Polaroid common stock, one or more calls have been bought and sold on each side, and both the striking prices (20 and 25) and the expiration dates (July and April) are different.

Before examining the various strategies involved in spreads, let's look at the basic principle behind all profits in spreads. We know that in most forms of investment we are rewarded if—and only if—we are right. If we buy a stock, for example, we profit only if it goes up in price. Similarly, if we sell a stock short, we gain only if it goes down. In my approach to trading options, *we don't take any position that involves only one side of the market.* We are never buyers *or* sellers only. We are buyers of something *and* sellers of something else at the same time. We are, therefore, to a great extent spared having to hope the direction of the market will favor our position. We try to position ourselves so that we profit whether the market goes up, down, or remains the same. The additional advantages of being on both sides of the market at the same time are that we may be able to predetermine our maximum possible loss in advance and we may be able to take a position that will assure us a profit within a wide latitude of price movement of the stock, both up and down. I refer to this latitude as the profit zone.

In spreads, there is a relationship between the premium (or price) paid for the buy side and the premium received for the sell side. For example, in the spread:

Bought 2 Polaroid July25 at 2¾
Sold 2 Polaroid April25 at 1¾

the premium on the calls bought (2¾ or $275) is one point (or $100 per call, as each call involves 100 shares of the underlying stock) more than the premium on the sell side(1¾ or $175). This one-point difference in price or premium is the spread. This spread will narrow, widen, or stay the same with the passage of time and the fluctuations in the price of the underlying stock (Polaroid common stock). And this narrowing, or widening, or failure to do either will determine our profit or loss in this spread.

In this case, we will profit if the spread widens; that is, if the original difference in price between the calls bought and the calls sold, of one point or $100, increases. The spread will widen if both sides of it advance in price but the buy side advances more. The spread will widen if both sides fall in price but the sell side falls more. The spread will widen if the buy side advances and the sell side remains the same or falls in price (or premium). The spread will also widen if the buy side remains the same and the sell side falls. It doesn't matter what causes the spread to widen; what matters is that it widens. Let's now see under what circumstances we may expect the spread to widen and deliver us our first profit.

7. Time Only Spreads

Time only spreads are spreads in which the terms of **the** calls bought and the calls sold differ *only* in the *time* of expiration. *In addition, the number of calls bought and sold is equal.* Here is an example of a time only spread:

Bought 2 Polaroid July25 at 2¾
Sold 2 Polaroid April25 at 1¾

The number of calls bought and sold is the same (2); the striking price on both the buy and sell sides is the same (25). The only difference in the calls themselves is that those on the buy side expire three months later than those sold. The premiums or prices are not the same but the premium is not a term of a call; it is the price paid for a call.

All of the following are examples of time only spreads:

Bought 6 General Motors April30 at 11¾
Sold 6 General Motors July30 at 13⅛

Bought 5 IBM October200 at 29
Sold 5 IBM April200 at 14⅜

Bought 7 U.S. Steel April50 at 7⅝
Sold 7 U.S. Steel July50 at 9⅛

Bought 3 Upjohn April40 at 2¼
Sold 3 Upjohn July 40 at 5

Despite the fact that all of the above are examples of time only spreads, they do not offer equal profit-making opportunities. In fact, some of them are a good bet to lose money. I think it was H. L. Mencken who said that most complicated problems have simple solutions. Perhaps the problem of trading listed options profitably can be simplified by selecting the best types of vehicles for profit from among the various available investment modes and then examining what to look for and what to avoid at the time the money is invested, while the position is held, and when it is liquidated. Let us begin this type of examination with the time only spread.

What to Look for in Time Only Spreads

GETTING IN

1. Sell the near expiration, buy the middle or far month.

The example, Bought 2 Polaroid July25 at 2¾ Sold 2 Polaroid April25 at 1¾, has an excellent chance to show a profit. Let's see why.

In the first place, time has been made our ally. When there is a difference in time until expiration, the calls bought should always have more time before expiration than the calls sold.

There are currently four expiration months or

maturities of any particular listed option. Listed options on any particular stock expire every three months; for example, January, April, July, and October in the Polaroid options in the above example. Another listed option might expire in February, May, August, and November. Only the nearest three maturities trade at any time. In the Polaroid example, April, July, and October options were available. The January (of the next year) maturity had not begun to trade and would not do so until the April option expired, toward the end of April. At that time, July, October, and January options would be available.

For convenience, we will refer to the three maturities which trade at any particular moment as the near, the middle, and the far maturities. If April, July, and October were currently trading, April would be the near maturity, July the middle, and October the far. Our first requirement in time only spreads is that we always sell the near month and buy the middle or far.

In the example given: Bought 2 Polaroid July25 at 2¾ Sold 2 Polaroid April25 at 1¾, we are assuming that this position was taken after the January maturity expired but before the expiration of the April; i.e., a time when the April maturity was, in fact, the near month.

2. In time only spreads the calls we buy and sell are always "out of the money" when we commit our funds.

An out-of-the-money call is a call whose striking price is higher than the market price of its underlying stock. The striking price of the calls bought and sold is 25 ($25 per share). Polaroid common stock is the underlying stock. Rule 2 simply means that in the example given Polaroid common stock must be selling in the market at a price *less than* $25 per share. If Polaroid common stock is selling for less than

$25 per share, the striking price of 25 will be higher than the market price of the underlying stock and calls with a striking price of 25 will be out of the money.

Figure 1 provides some insight into the reason why we always sell the near-month calls and why the calls must be out of the money when we take our position in this type of spread.

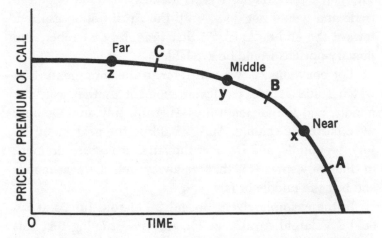

Fig. 1   Relative rates of premium decline of three different maturities of out-of-the-money call options with the same striking price, assuming fairly constant price of the stock. Note the accelerating rate of decline as expiration approaches.

Figure 1 is an approximation of the price movement of out-of-the-money option premiums with varying amounts of time remaining until expiration, assuming a fairly constant price for the underlying stock. Note that near-month out-of-the-money calls begin an accelerating decline in premium about two months prior to expiration. Therefore, about nine weeks prior to expiration is a good time to make this commitment. The closer to maturity, the less the risk.

All out-of-the-money calls are worthless at the time they expire: nobody would be willing to pay for the right to buy stock at a higher price than its market price (which, by definition, is less than the striking price in out-of-the-money calls) when there is no time left in the call until it expires. For example, an IBM April200 would be worthless the moment before it expired if IBM were selling for less than $200 per share. Anybody could buy it for less than $200 per share in the market and there would be no *time* left in the *call* during which the stock might rise.

But, and this is the significant point, out-of-the-money calls of *different* maturities do not lose their premiums at equal rates. The near-month out-of-the-money maturity loses its premium at a much more rapid rate than either of the other maturities. Figure 1, therefore, looks something like an airplane coming in for a landing: slowly descending, then dropping at a sharper angle, until it is rolling along on the ground.

Points x, y, and z represent the premiums of the near, middle, and far maturities of any out-of-the-money calls on the same underlying stock and of equal striking price—the Polaroid 25, for example. We would expect to pay a higher premium for a similar call with more time remaining until expiration because more time provides more opportunity for the stock to rise in price. A, B, and C are points equal in *time* from x, y, and z respectively. In other words, in the amount of time it takes the near expiration call to get to point A, the middle maturity is moving to point B and the far expiration is moving to point C. As can be seen from the figure, the near maturity has lost *much more* of its premium than the middle month which, in turn, has lost *somewhat* more of its premium than the far month, which, in turn, has lost *very little* of its premium. Equal amounts of time are affecting their premiums unequally.

Therefore, if we position a time only spread and sell the near month and buy the middle or far month, and their striking price is out of the money and stays out of the money, we may expect to gain more than we lose, for a net profit on the position. (And, as we will see shortly, we may be able to gain not only on the position as a whole but on both the buy and the sell side.)

Let's see why we expect to profit. In the example given:

Bought 2 Polaroid July25 at 2¾
Sold 2 Polaroid April25 at 1¾

we have seen that Polaroid common stock had to be selling at a price lower than $25 per share when we took the position. If Polaroid common stock did not climb to a price higher than $25 per share as we approached the expiration of the Polaroid April25 option, this option would begin an accelerating decline, as we saw in Figure 1. As x (Polaroid April25) approached point A, it would lose more of its premium (its price) than either y (the middle option, the Polaroid July25, in this example) would lose in moving to point B, or z (the far option—Polaroid October25, in this example) would lose in moving to point C.

Near the expiration of the Polaroid April25—for example, three weeks prior to its expiration—if Polaroid common stock were selling for, let us say, $23 per share, the Polaroid April25 might be selling for about ¼ ($25 per option on 100 shares of Polaroid common stock), while the

Polaroid July25 might be selling for about 2 ($200 per option), since the latter would still have sixteen weeks until its expiration and the market would place about this value on the chances for appreciation of a volatile stock like Polaroid during a period of this length.

If we wanted to cash in our position, we could sell our 2 Polaroid July25 options at 2 (and collect $400, ignoring commissions) and buy 2 Polaroid April25 at ¼ (and pay $50, again ignoring commissions) in closing transactions. We would receive a net of $350. We originally paid twice 2¾ for the Polaroid July25 calls (or $550) and we received twice 1¾ (or $350) for the 2 Polaroid April25 calls we sold when we took the position. We originally paid $200 more than we received; we now receive $350 more than we paid, for a profit of $150 on the spread, ignoring commissions.

We have taken this position in out-of-the-money calls. However, it must be understood that the more out of the money the call, the lower the premium. The lower the premium on the calls we sell the less our potential gain. A good rule-of-thumb compromise of safety vs. profit potential is that the price of the stock (Polaroid common stock, in this example) be about 80 percent of the striking price of the call, adjusted upward or downward for the time left until expiration of the near-month call. About nine weeks until the expiration of the Polaroid 80 percent of the striking price of 25, or a price of $20 per share for Polaroid common stock would be about right. The more time left until expiration, the more protection we would want and the more out of the money the call sold should be. This means that with more than nine weeks until expiration of the near call, the price of the Polaroid common stock, in this example, should be less than $20 per share.

3. Get at least a two-to-one "value" advantage.

Not only do near-month maturities decline fastest (if the underlying stock remains out of the money) but they also tend to be the most overvalued, thus making our profit even surer. One quick way to compare value is to compute how much per week the underlying stock would have to rise, by the time of expiration, in order for a buyer of the call to break even.°

(numerator)		(denominator)
Number of points stock must rise by the time of expiration of call in order for call buyer to break even °°	divided by	number of weeks until expiration of call °°°

Let's apply this formula to the example:

Bought 2 Polaroid July25 at 2¾
Sold 2 Polaroid April25 at 1¾

Let us assume these were the actual prices on February 21, 1975 and that Polaroid common stock was selling at 20½ (dollars per share). We know that the buyer of the Polaroid April25 paid 1¾ or $175 for the right to buy 100 shares of Polaroid common stock at $25 per share at any

° We are ignoring commissions and other costs in this section, but they will be included in the section that involves my own trading.

°° This is equal to the striking price of the call plus the premium of the call minus the market price of the underlying stock.

°°° As there are five business days in a typical week, one day equals 1/5 or .2 week.

I suggest that readers get the feel of these trades by making their own computations in the blank space provided below.

time until the April25 expired, a date toward the end of April 1975. The expiration date was the last Monday in April—April 28, 1975—but note that expiration dates of calls have changed since then. In order for this buyer to break even at the expiration date, the stock would have to be selling at 26¾ (ignoring commissions).

We have seen that all calls that are out of the money at expiration are worthless. Calls that are in the money (underlying stock selling at a *higher* price than the striking price of the call) are worth an amount equal to the market price of the underlying stock minus the striking price of the call, at expiration. At the last moment before expiration, with Polaroid selling at 26¾, the Polaroid April25 would have no additional value based on future prospects (time value) and would be worth 1¾. Thus, Polaroid would have to rise from 20½ to 26¾, or 6¼ points in 9.2 weeks (6.25 divided by 9.2 shows a rise of .6793 points per week).

Let's evaluate the Polaroid July25, using the same formula. Polaroid would have to rise to 27¾ at expiration, or 7¼ points, for the buyer of the Polaroid July25 at 2¾ to break even at expiration. 7.25 divided by 22.2 (the July call has 13 more weeks in it than the April) shows a rise of .3266 points per week.

Thus, the April25 needs a price rise of more than twice as much per week on this basis as the July25. Our rule of thumb in this value area is that we require at least twice as much "value" of the call we sell as compared with the call we buy, computed on this basis. With both time and value on our side, we are well on our way toward profit.

4. Don't pay more than 60 percent more for the calls you buy than you receive for the calls you sell.

We want to get a premium for the near-month calls we

sell that is as close as possible to the premium we pay for the calls we buy. This difference in premium—the spread— is the most we can lose (plus commissions and some pennies for the Securities and Exchange Commission fee) * in a time only spread if we liquidate both the calls bought and those sold at the same time. In the Polaroid example, if we'd received 2¾ for the April25 calls we sold (instead of 1¾) the spread, that is, the difference in price between the calls bought and the calls sold would have been zero and our risk of loss would have been reduced accordingly. But the near maturity call is never worth as much as a middle or far month of the same striking price on the same stock. This is obvious, since the middle and far months have greater time values. Because the middle and far months are always worth more than the near-month call, it is unusual to lose the full amount of the spread, that is the full difference in price between what you paid for the calls bought and what you received for the calls sold. Equally obvious, the closer in premiums the calls bought and sold, the less the total possible loss. (And the closer the spread, the less money we need to put up in order to make the investment.)

We have seen that the more out of the money the call we sell, the less the risk of losing money on the sale. But the more out of the money the call we sell, the lower the premium we receive and the less potential profit there is to be made. In order to avoid the wrong mix, I impose the condition that the premium of the calls bought may not be more than 60 percent more than the premium of the calls sold; this is the same as imposing the condition that the premium of the calls sold must be at least ⅝ (62½ percent)

---

* Paid only when selling, the SEC fee is one cent per $500 of sale proceeds or fraction thereof.

of the premium of the calls bought in time only spreads. This automatically avoids situations that are too "deep-out-of-the-money."

The premium of the Polaroid April25 is 1¾; the premium of the July25 is 2¾, or 57 percent more, and is therefore acceptable.

5. Don't sell calls with premiums of less than one dollar.

The potential gain on the spread is scaled down too far if the calls sold are too low-priced. In addition, if the calls sold net only a few dollars, not much profit can be made even if their premiums or prices decline to almost zero. Therefore, the gain on the spread would have to come primarily from the calls bought. We want to be in a position to gain from *both* sides of the spread.

6. Avoid trading only one low-priced call at a time if you can possibly afford to do so.

Commissions on a single low-priced call are relatively very high.

7. If both a middle and a far month satisfy all the conditions, sell the near month and buy the far.

This allows more time in which to realize a profit on the calls bought and allows for the possibility of covering (buying back) the calls sold at a profit and then selling calls on what had originally been the middle month, creating one profit and another time only spread. For example, if we'd taken the position:

Bought 2 Polaroid October25 at 3
Sold 2 Polaroid April25 at 1¾

and later bought 2 Polaroid April25 at ¼ in a closing transaction about three weeks prior to the expiration of the

The reader may want to compute this to become more familiar with the method.

April options, we might then have sold 2 Polaroid July25 options at 2¼, thereby putting ourselves into another time only spread:

Bought 2 Polaroid October25 at 3
Sold 2 Polaroid July 25 at 2¼

What to Look *Out* for in Time Only Spreads

GETTING IN

1. Always use limit orders; do not trade "at the market."

In buying and selling *stocks*, I recommend trading at the market. A market order instructs the broker to buy or sell at the best available price when the order reaches the point on the floor of the exchange at which the particular security is trading. Thus, he may buy at the offered price or sell on the bid, both of which may be considerably different in price from the last sale. In the case of a $40 stock, for example, I don't particularly mind if I pay an eighth or a quarter of a point or so more when I buy and get a similar amount less when I sell. When I've made up my mind to make the commitment I want to trade, and these small fractions are too insignificant to risk missing the market.

When I trade options, however, they are usually low-priced. A quarter of a point *is* significant in relation to a two- or three- or six-dollar option. In addition, markets in options are generally thinner than they are in the underlying stock. This means that it is harder, in general, to find as large a number of calls bid for and offered as can be found hundreds of shares of the stocks underlying the calls.

Market orders for several calls at one time would therefore tend to raise or lower prices in and of themselves.

Therefore, I always place a limit on what the options broker may pay or accept. As a general rule, options lag behind stock prices. This means that if the underlying stock begins to rise, the options on that stock will tend to rise slightly later (and at a slower rate) and fall slightly later (and at a slower rate) if the stock falls. This is an advantage for us, in that it helps us avoid missing markets and is another reason for not using market orders.

I usually limit my buy and sell orders to last-sale prices. However, if I am concerned about missing a market in a low-priced call, I simply add an eighth (in a rare case, maybe even a quarter) of a point to the last-sale price, but still limit the price I am willing to pay (and similarly offer calls at an eighth or possibly even a quarter of a point less than the last sale if I am a seller), but I never trade at the market; that is, I never place an order without limiting its price. I am sparing in adding an eighth or a quarter to last-sale prices of buy orders and taking a similar amount less when I sell. I find that brokers will often get you a better price than this adjusted limit but as often get you a bad price on a market order.

2. Avoid spread orders; trade the buy and sell sides as separate orders.

All spreads may be traded in a single spread order. That is, you may place a single order that requires both the buy and sell sides of the spread to be bought and sold together or neither side to be bought or sold. You might, for example, place a spread order to Buy 2 Polaroid July25 *and* Sell 2 Polaroid April25 at one point. This means that you don't care at what prices you buy and sell as long as the spread (the difference in price between the calls bought and sold) is one point (or less).

The rule here is simply to avoid placing spread orders, and the reasoning is simple. The broker on the floor will be able to get a spread order positioned for you, in general, only if the bid price on the calls you want to sell and the offered price on what you want to buy are equal to the spread *at the same time*. Therefore, if you want to take a position in a spread at the last sale differences in prices, you are likely to miss the market with spread orders, because of the fluctuations and the fact that other brokers who may trade either one side or the other will be able to exercise greater flexibility than your broker. In addition, the last-sale prices almost certainly do not represent bid prices on what you want to sell and offered prices on what you want to buy. Although the calls to be sold and those to be bought may trade through the last-sale prices several times, your broker will probably be unable to fulfill the spread order.

Let us say that you want to invest in the sale of 2 Polaroid April25 options and the purchase of 2 Polaroid July25 options at a spread of one point. Let's assume that the last sale of the April25 was 1¾ and the July25 last sold at 2¾. At the time the Polaroid April25 sold at 1¾ it might be quoted 1⅝ bid, offered at 1⅞; the July25 might be quoted 2¾ bid, offered at 2⅞. The spread order at one point would not be filled but two separate orders, Buy 2 Polaroid July25 at 2¾ and Sell 2 Polaroid April25 1¾, would have a good chance to be filled, at different times over a relatively short interval of the day.

Therefore, if I like the spread of the last-sale prices of two calls (because it meets all of the tests set forth above) I will enter a buy order and a separate sell order at these prices. If the market in the underlying stock is fairly flat (not especially strong or weak), I will probably get both orders filled, assuming they are not for too many calls. If the market shows particular strength or weakness, one side will be filled and I may wait for the other to be filled at the price chosen or adjust the order slightly in the direction of the market.

3. Never be a "naked seller" after the market closes.

A naked seller is a person whose position includes one or more options sold without any position bought in the underlying stock or any option on that stock. The principal reason for not being a naked seller is that all that can be gained (even if the option becomes worthless) is the amount for which you sold the option. But if the stock runs up in price, the option may appreciate many times over what you received for selling it. The risk/reward ratio is therefore unacceptable: you may lose much more than you can possibly gain. Therefore, I prefer to place both the buy and sell orders early in the trading day and at the same time. If the sell side is filled first, I make sure to have the buy side filled before the market closes even if this means paying slightly more than I'd originally wanted to pay.

4. Avoid oversold stocks and oversold markets.

Thus far, all of the elements required for taking a position in a time only spread and all those to be avoided required no knowledge of the stock market. This fourth factor does require judgment based on knowledge. However, even in the absence of informed judgment, we can apply a rule of thumb.

We would like to select a time only spread whose underlying stock remains about the same in price or even slightly declines after we make the commitment. This will tend to run out the clock or use up time on the near calls (the ones we sold). This will assure a profit as the calls sold will begin their final glide path toward the bottom line of Figure 1, valuelessness. At the same time, the calls bought will be declining less rapidly. This will enable us to close out the entire spread at a profit or to close out the sell side at a high profit rate. We may then, if we choose, keep the calls bought in the hope that a relatively small upside reaction in the underlying stock will provide a second profit. The net profits to be obtained in this way will usually be highly satisfactory on an annual basis, particularly in view of the limited risk involved.

The application of this phase of our strategy dictates the avoidance of stocks that are either about to make major rises or are highly volatile (subject to rapid, relatively large price moves in either direction). Slow movements will destroy the premiums of the calls we sold by using up relatively large chunks of time. Fast movement on the down side can yield a net profit on the spread or even, as we've seen, provide profits on both the buy and sell sides of the spread (by allowing us to buy back the calls sold at a profit and keep the calls bought for another profit if the stock rises somewhat), or by "averaging down," as we'll see. But a fast, sharp rise in the price of the stock can hurt us by moving up the price of the near-month call (and possibly getting us called upon to make delivery of the stock on the calls we sold) and at the same time leaving the stock ripe for a partial retracing of the upside move.

We will see how to deal with these contingencies later. However, it is prudent to try to avoid stocks that are ready to break out on the upside and to avoid oversold markets generally (markets that have recently had large declines). As a rough guide, I would recommend stocks that are more than 10 percent below their high for the last twelve months and preferably declining toward the middle of their price range over the past year, in markets that had not recently sold off more than 75 Dow Jones Industrial points from a previous top. This information is readily available in any brokerage office.

What to Look for in Time Only Spreads

ALONG THE WAY

The first objective is an acceptable profit on the entire spread (by selling the calls bought and buying the calls sold). If one presents itself, I would take it. However, often a profit is available on one side or the other at a time when there is not yet available an acceptable profit on the entire spread. The rule here is that we never accept a profit on only the calls bought, for this would leave us in a naked-sold position. We have already seen that this is to be avoided as an unwarranted risk/reward situation. (The maximum gain is the premium but the potential loss is unlimited.)

However, an opportunity for profit may present itself on only the calls sold. We have seen that in all markets except a strong up market in the underlying stock we may expect the premium of the calls sold to decline sharply as they approach expiration. By way of example, in the time only spread:

Bought 2 Polaroid July25 at 2¾
Sold 2 Polaroid April25 at 1¾

the underlying stock was selling at 20½ on February 21, 1975, when this spread was positioned.

On March 7, two weeks later, with Polaroid at 20 ⅞, the Polaroid April25 closed at ¾. The common stock had actually advanced slightly in price while the near all, racing toward oblivion, as in Figure 1, had lost more than 50 percent of its premium. A 50 percent or better drop in premium is one of the objectives I look for in calls I sell. If there were only about two weeks or so to expiration, I would have preferred to hold the calls to expiration in the hope of a 100 percent gain on the calls sold (and the saving of a commission) by simply letting them expire unexercised. They would be worth zero and the entire amount received for their original sale would be profit. But there were still 7.1 weeks until expiration, enough time for the common stock to rise, perhaps even into the money (above $25 per share), so I took this profit. As a rule, the point to watch for is an acceptable profit on the sell side.

The Polaroid July25 calls I had bought were declining at a much more leisurely rate and still had more than 20 weeks until expiration. A short time later the stock rallied and these calls were selling at an even greater percentage of profit than I'd realized on the calls I'd originally sold.

What to Look *Out* for in Time Only Spreads

ALONG THE WAY

About the only thing that might upset this spread, assuming it has been positioned in accordance with all of the suggestions outlined, is that the underlying stock (Polaroid common stock, in this example) rises above the striking price (of $25 per share). A sufficient rise above the striking price may get us called for delivery of the underlying stock. That is to say, whoever bought the calls we sold may now want to exercise them by giving us $25 per share and asking us to give them 100 shares of Polaroid common stock for either one or both of the calls we originally sold. We will see how to deal with this possibility when we consider what to look *out* for in getting out.

There are some who may want to avoid the possibility of being called for delivery, even if this means taking a small loss. I have never followed this course myself, and it is not recommended, but I know from experience with hundreds of clients when I was in the securities business that people react to the same circumstances in various ways. I have seen some who argue bitterly about the tax on a luncheon check blithely commit tens of thousands of dollars to the market. Others who make heavy commitments in their businesses may panic at the prospect of a two-point paper loss.

For those who want to get out if the stock rises above the striking price of the calls sold, some practical considerations: The premiums of both the calls bought and the calls sold will tend to rise as the price of the underlying stock rises. And time is still our ally. The longer it takes for the stock to rise above the striking price of the calls sold, the less these calls will rise in price or premium. Because less time remains until expiration, the "time" value of the call will be reduced; this means that the market will not put a high price on the possibility of a further rise in the price of the underlying stock when there is not much time for that possibility to materialize. There might even be a slight decline in the price of the calls as we saw on page 70. At any rate, we may, if we choose to avoid being called for delivery of stock, liquidate the entire spread (by buying the calls originally sold and selling the calls originally bought in closing transactions) at limit prices, not at the market, as suggested in #1 of "What to look out for getting in," even if this means taking a small loss. We will shortly look at alternatives to this course in the event the stock runs up beyond the striking price of the calls sold.

What to Look for in Time Only Spreads

GETTING OUT

The underlying stock will either be above the striking price of the calls when we liquidate our position, or it will not. If it is not above the striking price, we will almost certainly have a net profit on the calls sold. I look for a halving of the premium I got as a reasonable objective for closing out the calls sold. That is, I try to buy back the calls sold at half the premium I originally received. If this halving takes place within about two weeks of expiration of the calls sold, however, I tend to stay until expiration. At that time, if the stock is selling under the striking price, we've already seen that the call becomes worthless, and the entire premium we've received becomes the gross profit on the sell side.

We have already seen why we never leave ourselves in a naked short position. (The risk/reward ratio is unsatisfactory: we can gain only the premium received but we can take unlimited losses.) We therefore either close out the entire spread at an acceptable profit if we can, or close out only the sell side at an acceptable profit and continue to hold the buy side. My preference is to continue to hold the buy side for as short a time as will yield a profit, since this is a position that will profit us only if the market moves in one direction, up. If, however, the market moves lower when we are only on the buy side, I "average down" if the premium of the calls I originally bought declines 50 percent.

Averaging down works this way: In the example:

Bought 2 Polaroid July25 at 2¾
Sold 2 Polaroid April25 at 1¾

let's assume we've closed out the sell side at ⅞ (half the premium of the calls sold) when Polaroid was selling at 20⅞ but did not have an acceptable net profit on the entire spread. We therefore continued to hold the buy side. Let us assume that a week later the stock dropped in price to18⅞. When the Polaroid July25 is selling at a much lower price (premium) than when we originally bought it (I use half price as a rule of thumb) I would purchase either the same *number* of options already purchased (which was two) or, for even better probable results, approximately the same *number of dollars* worth of the option already purchased. At half the original price, you can buy approximately four options (taking commissions into account) for the same amount of money. If the stock then has a relatively small advance in price, this position will become profitable.

Averaging down, as this technique is called, is *not* recommended for *stock* purchases for several reasons:

1. In order to make averaging down work, the original purchase price must be sufficiently above the market price at the time averaging down is contemplated. The stock

most probably should not have been kept so long as to have permitted this loss to have occurred. If the stock has deteriorated in price to this extent it may be in a long-term down trend and require a long time to bottom out and rise enough to make averaging down work out to a profit.

2. Relatively large sums are needed.

3. If the commitments are made on a margin basis, it leaves one open to possible calls for additional margin if the stock continues to decline.

However, none of these reasons applies to averaging down in options.

1. The stock need not be in a major decline. Even a small price decline in the underlying security added to the "natural" decline in out-of-the-money options with the passage of time can produce relatively large declines in the price of the option. (This is the leverage factor working in reverse.)

2. Relatively small sums are needed.

3. One is not permitted to *buy* options on margin; they must be fully paid for, which makes a margin call on the buy side impossible.

Averaging down *is* therefore recommended on the buy side of options, as the leverage factor built into options can nudge us into a profit with a relatively small rise in the price of the underlying stock. This small rise need not be sufficient to put the stock back to the price it was selling at when we made the original purchase.

What to Look *Out* for in Time Only Spreads

GETTING OUT

1. About the only problem we will face in a properly selected time only spread is the possibility of being called

for delivery of 100 shares of the underlying stock for each of the calls sold, should the stock rise above the striking price of the calls. The overwhelming majority of calls are never exercised. I have never exercised a call, nor have I ever had one exercised against me, in all of the options trading I've done. In selecting our time only spread we have further minimized in several ways the possibility of being called for delivery. First, the calls we sold were out-of-the-money; that is, the price of the stock was less than the striking price of the call. Second, they had a limited time before expiration, reducing the possibility of the stock rising to a price where exercise of the call somebody bought (the April25 calls you sold) would be profitable to him. In addition, we picked a stock that wasn't oversold in a market that wasn't oversold. And, ideally, we should have tried to avoid selling calls on a volatile stock (one subject to sharp, fast price changes). Nevertheless, the possibility exists that if the stock rises above the striking price we may be called for delivery.

Should this happen, we will be given 100 times the striking price per call exercised. In the Polaroid example we've been using, we sold 2 Polaroid April25 calls at 1¾ or $175 per call. If, for example, we were being called for delivery of 100 shares of Polaroid we would receive $2,500. We would also keep the premium of $175 we'd received for the call we'd sold and it would cease to exist. We would then be obliged to deliver 100 shares of Polaroid common stock. At that point, we would have a choice:

a. We might take the $2,500 and the original premium of $175, buy 100 shares of Polaroid common stock in the market, deliver it (to the person exercising the call against us), and liquidate the rest of the spread, by selling the 2 Polaroid July25 calls we bought and buying 1 Polaroid

April25—the call we sold which was *not* being exercised—in closing transactions. I would recommend doing exactly this if it would give us an acceptable net profit. If not, we would have a second possibility:

b. We could take the $2,500 and use it to sell 100 shares of Polaroid common stock short. In selling stock short, we are selling stock we don't own in the hope of buying it back later at a lower price. Our broker would lend us 100 shares of Polaroid common stock (which we would have to replace later) and we would deliver this borrowed stock to the person exercising the call against us. Let's see how this might work out. Suppose it is April 15, Polaroid common stock has risen to 27½ (dollars per share), the April25 is 3¼ and the July25 is 4¾. Note that if we are called for delivery the call will usually come near the expiration of the call. There is no point in tying up funds exercising an option for a longer period than is necessary. This will normally give us a relatively long time in which to buy back the calls we originally sold, at a profit.

If we elect the first choice, we will go into the market and buy and deliver 100 shares of Polaroid at a cost of 27½, or $2,750. We received $175 for the call, plus $2,500 from the person exercising the call against us, a total of $2,675. This gives us a loss of $75 ($2,750 minus $2,675). If we liquidate the other call we sold by buying 1 Polaroid April25 at its current price of 3¼ (for which we originally received 1¾) we will lose $150. However, if we liquidate the 2 Polaroid July25 at the current price of 4¾ (for which we paid 2¾) we have a $400 profit. On the sell side, we have lost a total of $225 ($75 plus $150); on the buy side we have gained $400, for a total net gain of $175 ($400 minus $225) or enough to offset the commissions. Not the worst fate in the world considering that the market in Polaroid has gone sharply against us.

If we elect the second choice, we use the $2,500 to go short 100 shares of Polaroid, which our broker borrows for us. We deliver the borrowed stock and owe our broker 100 shares. We now have a paper loss on the Polaroid common of $250 (the difference between 25 and 27½) instead of an actual loss, as in the first choice. We also have an actual profit on the call exercised of $175. We have a paper profit on the 2 July25 calls of $400 and a paper loss on the 1 April25 of $150. We now hope to sell the 2 July25 calls, buy the 1 April25 call, and buy the 100 shares of Polaroid we owe the broker (at a lower price) so that the entire transaction yields a net profit. If the stock continues to rise we are almost completely protected, for the 2 July25 will continue to rise almost point for point with the stock, as will the 1 April25 call. (See Figure 2 on page 82 and note how in-the-money calls rise at an accelerating rate, increasingly approaching point for point with the stock, the deeper in the money the calls are.) As in the case of all stock sold short, we will have to pay any dividend payable to stockholders while we are short the stock, but we will not have to pay any interest to our broker on the stock sold short.

We do, however, have a further decision to make. The longer we take to cover (buy back) the Polaroid stock we are short, the more time is being used up on the July25 calls and the less time value remains in the call. We hope the Polaroid stock has a quick reaction; that is, sells lower (which is not altogether unlikely as it has moved from 20½ to 27½, or 34 percent, in a little over two months). This would permit us to close out the entire series of trades with

a net profit. If this does not happen, we are probably going
to have to accept a relatively small loss. However, although
the market has gone considerably against us, we are going
to have to take only a small loss, preserving our capital for a
better outcome the next time.

    2. Avoid market orders.

    3. Avoid spread orders.

Extra Point

There is one additional possibility that should be
examined. Suppose we had sold the Polaroid April25 calls
and bought the far month, October, instead of the middle
month, July. We would have an additional profit
opportunity:

> Bought 2 Polaroid October25 at 3⅝
> Sold 2 Polaroid April25 at 1¾

When we closed out the sell side at a profit near
expiration (by buying 2 Polaroid April25 at ⅞, for example),
we might continue to hold the October calls and then we
might have sold 2 Polaroid July25 calls, giving us an
acceptable profit on the April25 calls and another time only
spread, consisting this time of:

> Bought 2 Polaroid October25
> Sold 2 Polaroid July25

We would apply all of the same reasoning to this new
spread as we did to the April/July spread except that we
begin with a profit in this case. With good timing closing

Get the feel of these computations

out the April and July calls at profits, we might find the
Octobers have effectively cost us little or nothing. We
might then decide to sell the Octobers at a net profit on the
entire series of transactions, or hold it for an even greater
profit, if the stock rises.

How Much Does It Cost? *

The minimum amount of cash required to position the
time only spread is equal to the net amount of the buy side
(purchase price plus commission) minus the net amount of
the sell side (proceeds of the sale minus commission minus
the SEC fee). In the example given:

Bought 2 Polaroid July 25 at 2¾
Sold 2 Polaroid April 25 at 1¾

(2 times $275 plus $31.15   minus   (2 times $175, minus $28.85
equals $581.15)   minus $.01 equals $321.44)

the minimum margin   equals $259.71 ($581.15 minus $321.44).

In order to sell calls, we need to trade in a margin
account. The minimum requirements for opening a margin
account are governed by Federal rules and by brokerage
house rules, both of which are subject to change. In
addition, brokerage house rules differ widely from firm to
firm. It is essential that both sets of rules be understood
before you place any orders. As of early 1976, Regulation T
of the Federal Reserve Board required a minimum equity of
$2,000 to open a margin account, although you don't have
to use all of this amount on any particular trade.

* We will deal with the cost in terms of cash only, but securities having an equal
loan value would be acceptable.

In the Polaroid example above, a margin account is required and $2,000 in cash or in loan value of marginable securities would have to be deposited with the brokerage house in order to take this position, even though only $259.71 is actually required for the trade. For the same $2,000 we would, if we wanted to, be able to make a number of additional commitments or leave the balance idle.

All of the examples of margin requirements in this book presuppose the existence of a margin account. Some brokerage firms require more than $2,000 in order to open a margin account, so it is necessary to know the rules that will specifically apply to your own trading at the time you trade.

The minimum margin required for this trade and *all* other trades in this book are the minimums established by the options exchanges early in 1976.

However, firms which are members of the New York Stock Exchange, the American Stock Exchange, and other stock exchanges impose their own minimum margin requirements, which may be significantly higher than those of listed options exchange members. It is important to inquire what the rules are at a firm with which you contemplate doing business prior to trading, particularly as margin requirements may vary from firm to firm and from time to time.

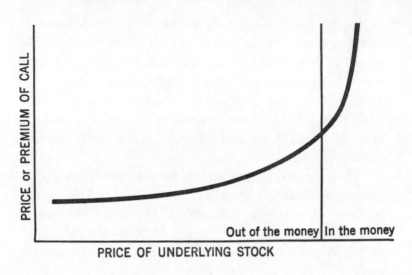

Out of the money | In the money

PRICE OF UNDERLYING STOCK

Fig. 2   Price of Underlying Stock

In Figure 1 we observed how the premium of an out-of-the-money call accelerates its decline toward zero as its expiration date approaches. Figure 2 represents the accelerated rise in premium of a call at a fixed point in time as its underlying stock advances in price. Note that the premiums of deep out-of-the-money calls rise slowly as the stock rises, while in-the-money calls rise in premium at a rate which increasingly approaches point for point with the stock.

8. Money Only Spreads with Equal Calls

Money only spreads involve calls on the buy side on which the terms differ from the terms of the calls on the sell side only in the amount of money required to exercise them; that is, their striking prices are different, but they expire at the same time. All of the following are examples of money only spreads:

Bought 3 General Motors April40
Sold 7 General Motors April45

Bought 2 IBM July200
Sold 2 IBM July220

Bought 4 Gillette July30
Sold 2 Gillette July25

There are many varieties of money only spreads, but they do not all offer equal opportunities for profit. Two specific spreads offer clear advantages over the others, and we should concentrate our attention on them.

Equal Calls, Same Maturity

The first of these opportunities involves an equal number of calls bought and sold, the same maturity month, and different striking prices. For example:

Bought 4 Upjohn July45
Sold 4 Upjohn July50.

At the beginning of this discussion of spreads I asked whether the reader would like to make a commitment in which the maximum gain could approach $500, the maximum loss be limited to about $100, with the chances of profit excellent. A typical example of how this can be done involves an equal number of deep-out-of-the-money options (striking price more than five points above the market price of the underlying stock) bought and sold in the *same* middle- or far-month maturity, with five-point differences in striking prices, and with the calls of the lower striking price the ones bought.

For example, before the April maturity expires, with Upjohn selling at $33 per share, such a spread might be:

Bought 4 Upjohn July45 at 2⅛
Sold 4 Upjohn July50 at 1¼.

All of the necessary elements for profit in this type of spread are present:

1. The same maturity for the calls bought and sold (July).

2. The maturity is a middle or far month (middle).

3. The number of calls bought and sold is equal (4).

4. The lower striking price is bought (45).

5. The calls are deep out of the money. The price of the underlying stock (33) is more than five points less than the lower striking price (45).

After we are satisfied that all these elements are present, there are other considerations that will determine whether or not to make the commitment. Let's now look at all of the factors that make for a profitable trade in this spread as well as what to look for and what to avoid at every stage.

The premiums of deep-out-of-the-money options are low. Two such options of five-point differences in striking prices may have premiums less than one point apart, whereas deep-*in*-the-money calls with a five-point difference in striking price would tend to sell at the full five points difference in price or premium. It is as if the reduced circumstances of both deep-out-of-the-money options have cast both of them on the same scrap heap despite their inherent potential differences.

In the above example, the Upjohn45 and the Upjohn50 calls are selling at a difference of ⅞ of a point, and we have positioned a middle month. Actually I took this position early in February 1975, with almost six months until expiration—lots of time. With this much time until expiration it was unlikely that these calls would sell much closer together in price even if the stock continued to fall in price. However, a widening in the spread was inevitable if the stock rallied. And if the stock rallied sufficiently, the spread might widen to as much as five points.

It should be obvious that an Upjohn45 can never be worth *less* than an Upjohn50 of the same maturity, for it permits a buyer to purchase the same number of shares (100) of the same stock (Upjohn common) for the same amount of time (until the expiration date) but for five dollars *less* per share. Shouldn't it therefore be worth something more than the call of a higher striking price, with the same expiration date? How much more? Anywhere from very little up to perhaps five points more.

Therefore, if we can buy the Upjohn45 at about the same price as the Upjohn50 we cannot lose very much on the transaction, and we can gain accordingly if the spread widens toward its potential of five points.

In the example given, from my own trading, there was a difference in premiums of ⅞ of a point but a potential difference of five points. The maximum potential loss was thus ⅞ of a point ($87.50 per call) and the potential gain was 4⅛ points ($412.50 per call), an attractive risk/reward ratio. In addition, there was ample *time* for the stock to rally, causing the spread to widen and a profit to result. Upjohn had sold for as high as 88¼ in 1974 and was a stock of excellent quality. It was selling in the thirties apparently because one of its drugs had been alleged to be harmful and there had been a selling panic, breaking the stock by about 20 points in a few weeks.

Upjohn is also a volatile stock, as could be seen by its broad range of prices (its high and low) over the past year. This is a desirable feature in this type of spread. We want a stock that can move up sharply and this requires volatility, while if it moves down sharply we don't stand to lose much. Two months after I took the position shown, the stock rallied to the point where the spread widened to 1⅞ points. An alert trader could have doubled his money (after commissions). As we'll see later, I was able to do even better, by taking additional profits, as suggested in the "Extra Points" material which concludes this section.

What to Look for in Money Only Spreads with Equal Calls

GETTING IN

1. We want to find a small difference in premium between two calls of the same underlying stock, same maturity and different striking prices. This will require that the striking price differences are the smallest offered in the particular underlying stock: 5 points in stocks selling under $50 per share; 10 points in stocks selling between $50 and $200 per share; and 20 points in stocks selling for more than $200 per share.

I suggest paying no more than a premium difference of 1 point for 5 points difference in striking prices, no more than 2½ points for 10 points difference in striking prices, and no more than 5 points difference in premium on a difference of 20 points in striking prices. The smaller the difference in price between the calls bought and the calls sold, the better the profit potential and the less the maximum possible loss.

2. We want as much time as possible before expiration of the calls, so that ample time is allowed for the spread to widen. I find the middle-month calls ideal in terms of offering not only enough time but also all of the other desirable features for this profit-making play. I recommend at least 20 weeks until expiration. This is a low-cost, low-risk situation and the profit potential is excellent, so I don't mind having a little money tied up a relatively long time.

3. We want volatility in the underlying stock, which means that we should avoid stocks that have little price movement. Quick, sharp thrusts will help us. I recommend

stocks whose highest price during the past twelve-month period was at least double their lowest price, and I would prefer a stock that also had exhibited some weekly ranges in price (difference between its high and low price for the week) of more than 5 percent of the price of the stock, during the previous thirteen weeks. *Barron's,* a weekly publication, can easily supply this information. It is available on newsstands every Saturday, and I usually spend a little time with it over the weekend.

4. We want to take positions in money-only spreads with equal calls whose underlying stocks have good upside potential. We will almost automatically be picking oversold situations, because calls with at least 20 weeks until expiration will be deep out of money and have as little price difference as recommended above, only if their underlying stocks have declined a great deal in price in a relatively short period of time.

While we will be attracted to stocks that have sold off considerably, we should try to avoid stocks whose companies have had severe reverses in prospects: it would not profit us to find candidates for bankruptcy. A well-financed, high-quality drug company like Upjohn, which receives a great deal of adverse publicity because one of its products becomes "controversial," can have a precipitous decline in the price of its stock without affecting the basic prospects of the company. But as more and more stocks have listed options available, the quality and long-term prospects of some may make them poor bets for this type of profit opportunity. All of the major services have quality ratings for stocks, and they are readily available through any customers' broker.

5. If both a middle- and a far-month maturity satisfy all the conditions, position the far month.

What to Look *Out* for in Money Only Spreads with Equal Calls

GETTING IN

1. Avoid market orders. This point was covered in detail in a previous chapter.

2. Avoid spread orders. This has also been treated in detail.

3. Don't sell before buying, for two reasons. As we have seen, we like to avoid being naked short. But, in addition, the call with the lower striking price (the one we buy) is more price sensitive. A change in price of the underlying stock will produce a bigger change in the price or premium of the call with the lower striking price. Therefore we should take our position in these calls first and then go into the market to sell the less price-sensitive calls of higher striking price and lower premium.

4. Don't sell calls with premiums of less than one dollar. This was discussed earlier but, to repeat: the maximum gain on a call sold is its premium—the lower the premium, the less to be gained. A point is reached where the potential gain is outweighed by the potential loss. In my opinion, less than one dollar for a call sold is unattractive.

5. Avoid overbought markets—markets that have run up the equivalent of 75 Dow Jones Industrial points from a previous low without any pause. I also suggest not position-ing this type of spread when the market is near the high end

of its long-term Dow Jones Industrial average (near Dow 1,000, in current terms).

6. Avoid trading only one call at a time if you can afford it, as the commissions on a single low-priced call are relatively very high.

What to Look for in Money Only Spreads with Equal Calls

ALONG THE WAY

1. I look for either an acceptable profit on the entire spread or an acceptable profit on the calls sold. If the stock rallies and the premium differential doubles, I would be inclined to take a profit on the entire spread. If the stock does not rally, I would look for a profit of 50 percent on the calls sold; that is, I would close out the calls sold (by buying them back in a closing transaction) at half the price or premium originally received for selling them.

A study of Figure 2 on page 82 will show why declines in the price of the underlying stock will have little effect in terms of changing the original spread between the calls bought and those sold. The calls of lower striking price (the Upjohn July45 calls, in the example given) that we bought will tend to preserve a greater percentage of their original premiums in the face of a drop in price of the underlying stock than calls of higher striking price. On the other hand, the lower-priced calls we sold (the Upjohn July50 calls in the example given) have fewer points to decline. These two factors will tend to offset one another and keep the spread, or price difference between them, relatively close to the original spread when we took the position (⅞ of a point, in the example given). On the other hand, price rises in the underlying stock will have an accelerating effect in widening the spread. As can be seen from Figure 2, as the price of the underlying stock approaches the striking price of the call, its premium begins to rise at a greater rate. What this means is that in the Upjohn example given, if Upjohn common stock rises from a price of $35 to a price of $36 per share, the Upjohn July45 might rise about ¼ of a point and the Upjohn July50 might rise about ⅛ of a point. However, if Upjohn goes from $46 to $47 per share, the Upjohn July45 might rise ⅝ or ¾ of a point and the Upjohn July50 (which is not yet in the money) might rise ⅜ or ½ a point. Thus, as the stock rises in price, the money only spread with equal calls begins to show a profit by increasing the spread between the calls we bought and the calls we sold.

If the stock does not rally and we close out the sell side (the 4 Upjohn July50 calls we sold) at an acceptable profit, we have a number of choices:

a. We may continue to hold the calls of the lower striking price that we bought and later sell them at a profit if the stock rallies and they appreciate sufficiently in premium.

b. We may average down, as with time only spreads, and later sell all of the calls bought on a rally in the stock.

c. We may continue to hold the calls we bought and go into another money only spread with equal calls if and when the July50 calls come back to their original or a higher price.

d. We may continue to hold the calls we bought (the July45 calls) and wait for a price on the July50 calls equal to the price we paid for the July45 calls and then sell an equal number of July45 calls at that price. This will give us another money only spread with equal calls, but we would now have another profit locked in, as the premium of the July45 calls would be considerably higher than the price we originally paid for them.

e. We may continue to hold the July45 calls and go into a time only spread by selling the April45 if it meets all the conditions for such a spread position, as set forth in the previous chapter.

What to Look *Out* for in Money Only Spreads with Equal Calls

ALONG THE WAY

1. One problem we may encounter along the way in a properly selected spread of this type is the possibility that no opportunity for profit on the entire spread and no profit opportunity on only the sell side presents itself. This is extremely unlikely but could occur if the natural erosion in the price of the calls sold (with the passage of time) were balanced by a slow enough rise in the price of the underlying stock. This would tend to keep the prices of both the calls bought and the calls sold at approximately constant prices.

2. The other problem that could occur is a decline in the price of the stock to a point at which we accept a profit on the calls sold (by buying them back in a closing transaction), followed by a further decline in the price of the stock right up to the expiration of the calls we had bought and are still holding (the Upjohn July45 calls, in the example given). This might happen in a long, unrelieved bear market.

However, it should be pointed out that in positioning these deep-out-of-the-money calls, their underlying stock had already suffered its own bear market. To further minimize the chance of loss resulting from continued weakness in the underlying stock (although the prevention of a bear market is admittedly beyond our control), we would avoid this type of spread as the general market rose toward the high end of its long-term range; that is, a Dow Jones Industrial Average of about 1,000. We would also avoid taking this type of position after a sharp, fast rise in the market; that is, we would try to avoid overbought markets.

What to Look for in Money Only Spreads with Equal Calls

GETTING OUT

The objectives in getting out are the various profit objectives mentioned "along the way." If we take a profit on the sell side and the stock continues its downward course, we may have to take a loss. We have already taken a profit of at least 50 percent of the premium on the calls originally sold. To help offset the prospective possible loss somewhat, we may be able to sell an equal number of near-month calls of the same striking price as the calls we are still holding. This will give us a time only spread. The calls we sell will probably expire unexercised, giving us a *second* profit and thirteen weeks in which to hope for an upturn in the stock.

Should the underlying stock fail to rally within a few additional weeks, we may want to sell an equal number of calls of the *same* maturity we are holding at a *higher* striking price (assuming all the conditions for the position are present). This will put us back into the same type of spread we had, a money only spread. We expect the calls we sold to expire unexercised and hope to bail out of the lower striking price calls at some, admittedly low, premium. This will give us a loss on the calls originally bought (the Upjohn July45 calls in the example) but *three* small profits to help offset this loss. This is a salvaging operation, not a recommended course, and it will come into play only in the unlikely event that the stock has a sustained downward move on top of its already sustained downward move at the time we took the original position.

This type of spread is not guaranteed to yield profits. There are no sure things in the market, although I think the odds are in our favor in this position. There may be occasional losses that will, I believe, be outweighed by fairly consistent profits. If, however, you find that you seem to be consistently unlucky with this spread or any other similar attempt to profit, don't force it. I would respectfully suggest you try to find a different way to invest your money and time.

When I was in the securities business I noticed there were some people who consistently took profits while others, given the identical advice, took losses. I cannot explain this phenomenon. It doesn't seem to be connected to age, sex, or education. I think it is a function of personality, but I don't really understand how it works. At any rate, I would advise those who lose consistently at a particular endeavor to consider giving it up in favor of other opportunities, rather than continuing to buck the trend.

What to Look *Out* for in Money Only Spreads with Equal Calls

GETTING OUT

If all of the above suggestions have been followed, there isn't very much to worry about. We know the maximum possible loss going in (if both sides of the spread are traded the same day).

1. If the stock rises, all of the calls will rise in premiums. But the premiums on the calls we bought will rise more than those of the calls we sold. Never simply sell out the calls bought and become a naked seller, as we've already seen. Liquidate the entire spread at a profit or close out only the calls sold at an acceptable profit and choose from among the possibilities "a" through "e" described above. I tend to accept a 50 percent premium on calls sold and am willing to stay long if there is ample time (at least thirteen weeks) until expiration.

2. Avoid market orders; trade only with limit orders.

3. Avoid spread orders. Use separate buy and sell orders.

Extra Points

If you can afford it, and if more than one opportunity presents itself, always diversify into more than one spread *if* that doesn't force you to trade only one low-priced call at a time. Single, low-priced calls require relatively high commissions. All of the opportunities presented in this book are designed to provide favorable risk/reward ratios. In order to minimize the effect of a possible loss in a particular investment, diversification is recommended. This will also help to move your capital faster and lessen the risk of being tied up in any single situation for an unduly long time.

How Much Does It Cost? *

As in the case of time only spreads, the minimum margin required for the money only spread with equal calls is equal to the net amount of the buy side (purchase price plus commissions) minus the net amount of the sell side (proceeds of the sale minus commissions minus the SEC fee).

In the example given, the minimum margin required would be $439.56.

Bought 4 Upjohn July 45 at 2⅛
Sold 4 Upjohn July 50 at 1¼

(4 times 2⅛	minus	(4 times 1¼
equals $850		equals $500
plus $47.05		minus $42.50
equals $897.05)		minus $.01
		equals $457.49)

$897.05   minus $457.49 equals $439.56

Thus, for $439.56 I had an extremely low-risk, high-potential profit situation.

---

* Assumes the existence of a margin account.

9. Money Only Spreads with Something Extra to Sell

On December 4, 1974, with Eastman Kodak selling at about 62, I took this position:

Bought 1° Eastman Kodak April70 6½
Sold 3 Eastman Kodak April80 4

If, at expiration, on April 28, 1975, Eastman Kodak were selling between zero and $70 per share, *all* of these calls would be worthless and I would profit by the difference between what I received for the calls I sold and what I paid for the call I bought: 3 times $400 equals $1,200 minus 1 times $650 equals $550 (minus commissions and an SEC fee).

If, at expiration, Eastman Kodak were selling between 70 and 80, I would have a profit of $550 plus $100 per point

---

° One call has a relatively high commission but (a) this is particularly true for *very* low-priced calls, and (b) partially covered calls require much additional margin, and I didn't want, at that time, to tie up the funds necessary to double the position.

above 70. The April80 calls would be worthless, but the April70 calls would begin to take on value in direct relation to how much above 70 the stock was selling. At expiration there would be no additional time value to consider.

Thus, the point of maximum profit at expiration would be $80 per share for Eastman Kodak. The profit would be $550 plus $1,000, or $1,500 (minus commissions and some pennies for the SEC fee). Above 80, however, the three April80 calls sold would begin to take on value at a rate of $100 per call per point and the April70 calls would continue to gain value at the rate of $100 per point. This spread position would therefore be losing a net of $200 per point above $80 per share for the stock. This net loss would be occurring at a point of plus $1,550 on the position. We would therefore break even, ignoring commissions, at 87¾ and lose $200 per point above 87¾, at expiration.

This may be summarized as follows:

	Price of Eastman Kodak at Expiration	Profit/Loss *
	0-70	plus $550
	70-80	plus $550 plus $100 per point
Bought 1 EK April70 6½	80	plus $1,550
Sold 3 EK April80 4	above 80	plus $1,550 minus $200 per point
	87¾	break even
	above 87¾	minus $200 per point

* Minus commissions and a small SEC fee.

With Eastman Kodak selling at 62 on December 4, this spread would show a profit if the stock stayed within a broad range of zero to 87¾ per share until April 28. I call this range the profit zone. In other words, for me to have lost money, Eastman Kodak would have had to have risen more than 41.53 percent within 20.6 weeks, more than 2 percent a week. (Actually, it did. One of the strongest stocks in a surging market, Eastman Kodak rose to an astonishing 95⅝ before the April calls expired, but I was nevertheless able to take a good profit on the sell side and a small profit on the buy side as well.) Before we see how profits may be taken prior to expiration, let's look more closely at the characteristics this type of spread should have.

The money only spread with something extra to sell is, not surprisingly, akin to the money only spread with equal calls. In both types, the maturity date of the calls bought and sold is the same. In both, the lower striking price call is bought, the higher striking price call sold. Also, the difference in premium between the two calls is a small percentage of the full difference in striking prices.

The major differences in the two spreads are that in this type we would like less time until expiration, less volatility, and less upside potential for the stock. In fact, had I known then what I know now I would have positioned an equal number of calls on each side (a money only spread with equal calls) and taken a bigger profit with a smaller investment (because less margin would have been required, as we'll see) and less risk. This was one of my earliest trades; I was still experimenting with my method, and learning more and more all the time.

Regardless of the price direction of the underlying

stock, the better-value, lower striking price calls tend to rise more and fall less than the higher striking price calls sold. If the stock remained fairly stable in price or declined even slightly, the calls sold would deteriorate rather rapidly, as we saw in Figure 1. In this instance, the market in Eastman Kodak backed and filled after I took a position in this spread. Twenty days later, with Kodak off about two points, the Eastman Kodak April80 calls had lost more than half of their premiums. This met the profit objective of 50 percent I look for in closing out calls sold, and I bought them in at 1 15/16 on December 24. The buy side also netted a profit, as we'll see in detail later. The point to be made is that even though this spread was improperly set up (it did not fully meet all the criteria for this type of spread but would have been a natural money only spread with equal calls) and the stock actually traded out of the profit zone before the expiration of the calls, the arithmetic of the position (the width of the profit zone, the ratio of the premiums of the calls bought and sold, and the ratio of premium difference to striking price difference) was good enough to provide a number of chances for profit.

It should be obvious that the ratio of calls bought to calls sold may be varied. Instead of a 1:3 mix, which was the proportion I selected, let's look at a 1:2 mix:

	Price of Kodak at Expiration	Gross Profit/Loss
	0-70	plus $150
	70-80	plus $150 plus $100 per point
	80	plus $1,150
Bought 1 Kodak April 70 at 6½	above 80	plus $1,150 minus $100 per point

Sold 2 Kodak April 80 at 4   91½   break even
                                      above 91½   minus $100
                                                              per point

The mix to be selected will take account of potential profit, the width of the profit zone, and the amount of money to be put at risk. If there is an opportunity to close out the calls sold at a price 50 percent or less than the original premium I received, and there is sufficient time left (more than thirteen weeks until expiration) so that a rally in the price of the stock may nudge the calls bought into profits (either by continuing to hold the calls bought or averaging down), I close out the calls sold. If either of these conditions is not present, I look for an acceptable profit on the entire spread and close it out. Let's now look at the specifics.

What to Look for in Money Only Spreads with Something Extra to Sell

GETTING IN

1. As with spreads with calls of different striking prices, same maturity, and an equal number of calls bought and sold (money only spreads with equal calls), we want as little difference in premium as possible between the calls bought and sold. I look for two conditions: no more than a 1-point difference in premium on a 5-point difference in striking prices (20 percent or less) and no more than a 25 percent difference in a 10- or 20-point difference in striking prices; and because of the greater risk of being only partially

covered, (we have sold more calls than we bought and have thereby increased our risk) I would like the premium on the calls sold to be at least 62½ percent of the premium of the calls bought. In the Eastman Kodak example, I got only 61.54 percent.

2. We want at least two dollars for the calls sold. Downside gains are more difficult and time-consuming, and commissions are relatively higher in lower-priced calls.

3. As little time to expiration of the calls as possible. I recommend no more than 20 weeks. There was slightly more time in the Eastman Kodak example.

4. A fairly stable stock. High volatility hurts us if the stock rises out of the profit zone. We are also required to put up more money if the stock rises. (This will be discussed in detail in the section on costs.)

5. The underlying stock should not be too close to its twelve-month low. This was flagrantly violated in the Eastman Kodak example. By going over this checklist of criteria for this type of spread we would have been led toward the best profit-making opportunities (money only spread with equal calls) and away from error. These checklists were not as clear before the experiments as after, however.

6. An appropriate mix. By this I mean that we will want a wide profit zone, few excess calls sold, and as little risk as possible. These factors have to be traded off somewhat, and it becomes an individual choice. The more excess calls sold, the more money is originally needed, and the more money must be put up if the stock rises and there is a greater risk of loss if the stock rises sharply. I am comfortable with a 1:3 mix as in the Eastman Kodak example, if all the other elements for a successful trade are present. I would begin to

feel uncomfortable with a greater preponderance of calls sold. The excess of calls sold adds a psychological pressure. Most investors can buy a stock and see it go down a couple of points with equanimity. However, if they sell a stock short and it rises a couple of points they tend to be considerably less calm. The excess of calls sold is analogous to a short position, and a rise in premium will affect different people differently.

What to Look *Out* for in Money Only Spreads with Something Extra to Sell

GETTING IN

1. Trading calls at the market and using spread orders is not recommended, as we've seen (pages 64 to 67).

2. We have also seen why it is safer to buy the calls first and then sell (page 89).

3. Highly volatile stocks are to be avoided. A sharp, upside move is the only upsetting possibility, and we want to minimize this chance for loss by avoiding volatile stocks. We have already seen a rule-of-thumb approach for finding volatile stocks (pages 87 to 88). We must make sure that we avoid these characteristics in the underlying stock for this type of spread. These criteria may be adjusted somewhat as time to expiration of the calls varies. The closer we are to expiration the more risk we may take with this element.

4. We want to avoid oversold stocks and oversold markets. The same reasoning applies here as we used with time only spreads (pages 67 to 68).

What to Look for in Money Only Spreads with Something Extra to Sell

ALONG THE WAY

1. My first objective is an acceptable net profit on the entire spread. What is acceptable is a matter of individual choice. In making the decision, I annualize the net profit. As we will see later in the chapter on taxes, there is what I consider to be an anomaly in the present tax laws that works against profits on listed calls sold. These profits are treated as regular income and not capital gains, which is bad enough. What is worse is that losses on listed calls bought may not be subtracted from gains on listed calls sold, as is the usual procedure with securities. Losses on listed calls bought are treated as subtractable from regular income up to the annual limit of $1,000 and beyond that limit they may be carried over to a following year; they may not be set off against gains on listed calls sold. A number of tax strategies will be discussed later but until this is changed or clarified by the courts or the legislature it is prudent to minimize the risk of loss as much as possible. The acceptance of profits and the avoidance of losses is my way of doing that. I am therefore inclined to accept smaller profits than might be warranted. These "smaller profits," however, when compounded and annualized, amount to extremely impressive gains.

2. If an acceptable net profit on the entire spread does not present itself, I look for an acceptable net profit on the calls sold. As we have seen, I would not take profits on only the calls bought because that would leave me in a naked sold position, an extremely unacceptable risk/reward posi-

tion. My own preference is to take a profit on a premium decline of 50 percent on the calls sold unless it occurs very close (about two weeks) to expiration, in which case I am inclined to ride out the calls sold to expiration in the hope of a 100 percent gross profit on them, as well as the saving of a commission in closing them out.

If I liquidate the sell side at an acceptable profit I am willing to accept a very small profit on the calls bought at the earliest opportunity. This is because I am now on only one side of the market (a buyer) and can therefore profit only if the market moves in one direction (up). A good profit already pocketed has a calming effect, but a position on only one side of the market is contrary to the underlying principle of my method of trading and must be reversed at the earliest available opportunity for profit. If necessary, I will average down, as described earlier, if the premium on the calls I bought is halved, and again look for the first opportunity to liquidate at a profit.

What to Look *Out* for in Money Only Spreads with Something Extra to Sell

ALONG THE WAY

1. Nothing can upset us if the underlying stock declines in price, for our profit zone extends to a price of zero on the downside. Only a fast, sharp upside move in the stock can jeopardize our profit. And the earlier it happens, the greater our problem. In the example:

Bought 1 Eastman Kodak April70 at 6½
Sold 3 Eastman Kodak April80 at 4

if Kodak rallies from a price of 62 to a price of 75 a few days before expiration, the Kodak April70 will be selling at about 5⅝ and the Kodak April80 will be under a dollar, for a handsome net profit. But the same move in the stock before Christmas, with four months until expiration, would have put the Kodak April70 to perhaps 10½ and the Kodak April80 to about 6⅜, for a net loss.

Such a move is, of course, unlikely if we selected our spread in accordance with all of the criteria suggested, but it is possible. Should it occur, we have three choices:

a. We may continue to hold the position and hope for a reaction (in this case, a decline in the price of Eastman Kodak common stock) which, with the passage of additional time, will erode the premiums of the calls sold (as a percentage) more than the loss on the call bought. We have also sold more calls than we bought so our profit on three calls and our loss on one call may well give us a net profit.

b. We may lighten our position in a mid-course correction. I have never used this kind of evasive action but the possibility should be considered. It may be effected by buying in one or more of the calls we have sold (at a loss) or adding one or more calls to the Eastman Kodak April70 call we have bought. Either of these moves, by changing the mix, limits the potential loss should the stock continue its rise, but it also narrows the profit zone.

c. We may decide on a maximum loss we are willing to accept and liquidate the entire position if that point is reached. This course should be considered. The strict limitation of losses preserves capital and allows for a comeback on subsequent trades. We expect losses will not occur often. If they are not allowed to become prohibitive we will have ample opportunities for net profits. Riding out a loss can produce a much bigger loss and reduce capital to a point of greatly impaired usefulness as a vehicle for gains. It requires discipline to accept a loss, but bucking a trend can be expensive.

2. Should the price of the underlying stock rise, we will be required to put up more money, as we will see in detail when we consider costs. The general principle involved is that we have deposited collateral which assures our performance with respect to a call for delivery on the excess number of calls we have sold. Should the stock rise in price, additional collateral is required.

What to Look for in Money Only Spreads with Something Extra to Sell

GETTING OUT

The profit objectives in getting out have already been covered along the way.

What to Look *Out* for in Money Only Spreads with Something Extra to Sell

GETTING OUT

The same considerations apply here as were discussed in money only spreads with equal calls.

Extra Point

Should we get an opportunity for an acceptable profit on the calls sold we may decide to buy in only the excess calls sold. This will put us into a money only spread with equal calls and give us an opportunity for additional profits with limited risk. For example, in the spread:

Bought 1 Eastman Kodak April70 at 6½
Sold 3 Eastman Kodak April80 at 4

I might have (if I'd known more at the time) closed out at a profit only 2 of the calls sold, at 1 15/16. This would have put me into the position:

Bought 1 Eastman Kodak April70 at 6½
Sold 1 Eastman Kodak80 at 4

In addition to a gross profit of $412.50 on the two calls closed out (2 times 4, or $800 minus 2 times 1 15/16, or $387.50 equals $412.50) this position would have provided an opportunity for an additional gain of 7½ points or $750 on the resulting money only spread. That is, the April70 and the April80 calls have a potential price difference of 10 points, or $1,000, but we paid a difference of only 2½ points, or $250 (6½ minus 4).

As the Eastman Kodak April70 cost only 2½ points more than the April80 (and, as we've seen, it can *never* be worth *less* than the April70) I would have been in a position where all of the profit I'd already realized couldn't be taken away from me. But if Kodak rallied (as it actually did), the spread between the April70 and the April80 might have widened to its full 10 points (as it did) and I would have had another 7½ points of profit to add to the already realized 4⅛ points, a gross of $1,162.50. The money only spread would have required only $250 plus commissions and would have yielded a $750 gross profit. This free ride in the right direction should have been considered.

How Much Does It Cost?

In figuring the minimum amount of money required for money only spreads with something extra to sell, the position is treated as if it were composed of two parts:

Bought 1 Eastman Kodak April70 at 6½
Sold 3 Eastman Kodak April80 at 4

Part I: Bought 1 Eastman Kodak April70 at 6½ Sold 1 EastmanKodak April80 at 4
This is a money only spread with equal calls.
Part II: Sold 2 Eastman Kodak April80 at 4
This part consists of 2 naked calls sold.

The minimum amount of money required for the position is the sum of the requirements for the two parts. The minimum required for Part I, as we've seen, is the net amount of the buy side ($650 plus a commission of $25) minus the net proceeds of the sell side ($400 minus a $25 commission minus $.01), which equals $299.99.

The minimum required for each call in Part II equals 30 percent of the market price of the underlying stock (62) times $100 minus the difference between the striking price of the call (80) and the market price of the underlying stock (62) times $100, minus the proceeds of the call, with a minimum of $250 per call.

Each call would therefore require a minimum of 30 percent of 62 times $100 or $1,860 minus (80-62 times $100, or $1,800) minus ($400 minus commissions). As this is an amount less than $250, each call would require the minimum of $250. The total original minimum amount (under the rules of the exchange, although brokerage houses might impose a minimum greater than the exchange minimum) needed for the position would be $299.99 plus $500, or $799.99.

However, any position that contains an excess of calls sold requires additional money to be supplied if the market in the underlying stock rises. This is similar to the requirement for additional funds for stock sold short. One of the three calls sold is considered to be fully covered by the call bought; the other two are considered to be not covered, or naked. The calls that are not covered at all (completely uncovered, or naked) are refigured at the close of each trading day and if the stock rises in price, additional collateral, or maintenance margin, may be required.

Thus, if Kodak closed at 70, Part I would not require any additional funds. Part II would be refigured. That is, each of the two calls would need 30 percent of 70 times $100, or $2,100 minus the difference between the striking price and the market price times $100 (80-70 times $100, or $1,000) minus the $400 premium of the call received. $2,100 minus $1,000 minus $400 equals $700 per call needed, or a total of $1,400. As $250 per call had already been deposited when the position was originally taken, the position would require an additional $900 if the stock closed at 70.

Before we leave this part of the discussion, it should be noted that the above requirements are the minimums. Some firms require a 40 or 50 percent figure instead of 30 percent if the account is worth less than $50,000. This adds greatly

Use this page for computation

to the amounts originally required and requires relatively larger sums if the market in the underlying stock rises. Many firms also often require a higher minimum than the $250 indicated; $400 is a current favorite. It should be noted that if the market goes in a favorable direction (in this case, if Eastman Kodak moves lower), funds would be released by the use of the same formula when the account was refigured at the close of the trading day.

The point that should be clear is that naked calls sold may require large cash reserves beyond the original need. Calls bought, on the other hand, are paid for in full and do not need additional funds regardless of the movement of the market.

10. Not-Only-But-Also Spreads (Money *and* Time)

This type of spread involves the buying and selling of calls on the same underlying stock which are different *not only* in time (expiration date) *but also* in money (striking price). Some examples of not-only-but-also spreads are:

Bought 3 IBM April220
Sold 2 IBM October 200

Bought 5 Eastman Kodak July80
Sold 7 Eastman Kodak April90

Bought 2 Gillette October35
Sold 2 Gillette July30

In spreads of this type, I require all of the following criteria:

1. An equal number of calls bought and sold.

2. The striking prices must be five points apart, and I always sell the lower striking price and buy the higher, but I take a position in this type of spread only when:

a. there are less than nine weeks until expiration of the near month and

b. the premium of the calls sold is higher than the premium of the calls bought and

c. the price of the underlying stock is equal to or less than the lower striking price.

3. The calls sold are always the near month and the calls bought are a middle month.

Let's look at an example from my own trading that satisfies all of these criteria. With Kennecott Copper common stock at 35 on March 5, 1975, I took this position:

Bought 3 Kennecott July40 at 2⅛
Sold 3 Kennecott April35 at 2¾

An equal number of calls were bought and sold (3). I believe this is the best mix in terms of risk/reward and profit *vs.* investment. The striking prices are five points apart (40 and 35). We have already seen that stocks under $50 per share have minimum striking price differences of five points. We want to be in striking prices that are different but as close as possible; five points was the smallest difference in striking prices then available. We are therefore choosing to be in calls of relatively low-priced underlying stocks. We want to limit the potential rise in the price of the underlying stock and lower-priced stocks will tend to rise fewer points than higher-priced stocks. The near-month,. lower striking price calls were sold; the middle-month, five-point higher striking price calls were bought, and there were less than nine weeks until the expiration of the near-month calls. The premium of the calls sold (2¾) was higher than the premium of the calls bought (2⅛), and the price of the underlying stock (Kennecott Copper was selling at 35) was equal to or less than the lower striking price.

We know from Figure 1 that near-month out-of-the-money calls begin their accelerating declines at about nine weeks before expiration, so we are inclined to sell them. We thus put time on our side. It is also a fact that, at about this time, calls in the middle month with a five-point higher striking price tend to rise equally with the near-month five-point lower striking price call (if the stock rises) and decline less (if the stock declines). It is also true that the near-month lower-price call will often sell at a higher premium. This combination of factors offers an excellent opportunity for profit.

If the price of the underlying stock stays about the same or declines, the near-month call will lose a much higher percentage of its premium than the middle-month call. This will result either in an acceptable profit on the entire spread or an acceptable (50 percent) profit on the calls sold and an opportunity for a second profit later on the calls bought, with or without averaging down.

If the price of the stock rises, the calls on both sides tend to rise about equally. The difference in premium that we obtained originally will more or less cover the commissions, and we will come out about even.

However, there is the possibility, if the stock rises, that we may be called for delivery on the calls sold. We know that the majority of calls are never exercised. However, if we are called for delivery we may use the money offered

(100 times the striking price per call) to buy the stock in the market and liquidate the entire spread, or we may use the amount tendered as collateral and sell 100 shares of stock short for each call exercised against us. This strategy has been covered in the material on what to look out for getting out of time only spreads on pages 74 to 78.

What to Look for in Not-Only-But-Also Spreads

GETTING IN

The necessary features of this type of spread have been listed above: less than nine weeks until expiration of the near-month calls; a five-point lower striking price and a higher premium for the near-month calls; and a price for the underlying stock that is not higher than the striking price of the near-month call. In addition, we don't want an upside breakout (a sharp, upward move in the price) of the underlying stock, so I look for low volatility in the underlying stock. I also prefer a price that is declining into the middle of the stock's range (its high and low) for the previous twelve-month period.

What to Look *Out* for in Not-Only-But-Also Spreads

GETTING IN

The same considerations apply here as were set forth in connection with time only spreads. This is not surprising, as this spread may be thought of as a variation of a time only spread.

What to Look for and Look *Out* for

ALONG THE WAY AND GETTING OUT

I apply the same reasoning as for time only spreads. It might be useful to try to work out that reasoning before checking the text.

In the example given: Bought 3 Kennecott July40 at 2⅛ Sold 3 Kennecott April35 at 2¾, the stock weakened somewhat over the near term. On March 12, one week after I took this position, with Kennecott at 34¼, the Kennecott April35 had been reduced by the passage of time and the slight weakness in the stock; it was selling at 50 percent of the premium I received for it. I was able to cover in some calls at 1⅜. The July40, however, had preserved most of its value. I closed out the sell side and continued to hold the buy side (the Kennecott July40 calls) in the expectation of another profit.

Extra Point

If the stock rallied, I intended to try for a third profit by selling an equal number of Kennecott *April*40 calls. This would put me into a time only spread position: Bought 3 Kennecott July40 Sold 3 Kennecott April40.

I subsequently went into this spread, expecting the April40 calls to expire unexercised, which would allow me to keep the entire net proceeds of the sale as a profit and to give me the Kennecott July40 calls for approximately nothing after subtracting the two profits received on the sell side. If Kennecott then rallied, there would have been an opportunity to take a third profit on the long side before the July calls reached a point of accelerated decline, about nine weeks prior to expiration.

There also might have been the possibility of a fourth and a fifth profit in this spread. Shortly before the expiration of the April40 call, they became virtually worthless and I nailed down a second profit. A later rally in the stock might have provided an opportunity to sell 3 July45 calls (there was not yet a 45 call trading in Kennecott, but if the stock rallied enough there would be). The time to take this position would be at a point where there was a profit in the July40 calls. This would create a money-only spread with equal calls. From that position, as we saw, it is possible to take a profit on both the buy and the sell sides. I might have decided to take the profit on the July40 (the third profit) and buy an equal number of Kennecott October (or January calls) and keep this process going indefinitely.

How Much Does It Cost?

The position, Buy 3 Kennecott July40 2⅛ Sell 3 Kennecott April35 2¾, required a minimum original margin of the difference in the striking prices minus the difference in the premiums per call, or $1,312.50, plus the commissions.

11. Butterfly Spreads

I learned about the butterfly spread from my customers' broker. The butterfly spread involves the selling of two calls and the buying of one call of lower striking price and one call of higher striking price on the same underlying stock, all of which expire at the same time. Here is an example of a butterfly spread based on actual closing prices for April 2, 1975:

IBM closed at	Buy 1 IBM October160 54
203¾	Sell 2 IBM October180 39½
	Buy 1 IBM October200 26

The maximum possible loss in this position is $100 (plus commissions) if liquidated at the same time, and the maximum possible gain is $1,900 (minus commissions). This includes all prices for IBM from zero to infinity.

In this spread, ignoring commissions and other minor costs (a total of $.16 in SEC fees), we have paid $5,400 for the IBM October160 and $2,600 for the IBM October200, a total of $8,000.* We have received $3,950 for each of two

---

* We should not confuse these premiums with the amount of margin necessary to take this position. In this case, minimum margin for the entire spread, involving four calls which control more than $81,000 worth of stock, is $2,100.

calls, a total of $7,900. Thus, we have paid $100 more than we received and this is our maximum possible loss.

If, on the expiration date of these spreads (the last Monday in October), IBM were selling at $160 per share or less, all of these calls would be worthless and our loss would be $100. If IBM were selling between $160 and $180 per share at the expiration date, the IBM October160 would be worth $100 for every point above $160 per share. At a price of 180 for IBM at expiration, our IBM October160 would be worth $2,000 and the other calls would be worthless, giving us a $1,900 profit.

Above $180 at expiration, we would gain an additional $100 per point on the IBM October160 we bought but lose $200 per point on the 2 IBM October180 calls we sold. This would give us a net loss of $100 per point between a price of 180 and 200 for the stock, at expiration. At a price of 200, we would have lost $2,000. This would give us a net loss of $100 as we would have been ahead $1,900 at a price of $180 per share.

Above $200 per share, we would gain $100 per point on the October160 we bought and an additional $100 per point on the October200 we bought but lose $200 on the 2 October180 we sold. This would give us a net of no gain/no loss. Thus, above 200, we would remain in a net minus $100 position. This may be summarized as follows:

Price of IBM at expiration of calls	Net gain or loss of butterfly spread *
under $160	minus $100
$160-$180	minus $100 plus $100 per point
$180	plus $1,900
$180-200	plus $1,900 minus $100 per point
$200	minus $100
above $200	minus $100

An interesting additional profit opportunity presents itself should we be called for delivery on one or both of the IBM October180 calls we sold. If we are called for delivery of 200 shares and use the cash we are given as collateral with which to go short 200 shares, and deliver the 200 shares we borrow against our short position, our position becomes:

Bought 1 IBM October160
Short 200 IBM at 180 plus $7,900 for the two October180 calls, which is now ours to keep
Bought 1 IBM October200

If, at expiration, IBM is selling above 200, our loss is still only $100 plus commissions. However, if IBM is selling under 180, we will have a profit of $1,900 as anticipated, *plus* an additional $100 per point for every point IBM is selling below 180. If, for example, IBM is selling at 165 at expiration, the IBM October200 is worthless, and we lose its

* Not including commissions and the SEC fee.

full purchase price of $2,600. The IBM October180 premiums we have already kept, a total of $7,900. The IBM October160 is worth $500 and we paid $5,400, a loss of $4,900. Minus $2,600 plus $7,900 minus $4,900 equals plus $400. This is what we anticipated when we took this position. However, we may now cover the 200 shares of IBM we are short at a profit of 15 points, for a profit of an additional $3,000, a total of $3,400 profit minus commissions and the few pennies for the SEC fee. (We also could have calculated this profit by adding to $1,900 the $100 per point below 180 we gain on covering our short position (180-165 equals 15), 19 plus 15 equals 34. If IBM were selling at 152, our profit would be $1,900 plus $2,800, or $4,700 (minus commissions and the SEC fee).

Prior to expiration, the passage of time and fluctuations in the price of the stock will affect the calls unequally. Should IBM decline in price, the October160 will tend to preserve a greater percentage of its value than the October180. In addition, more dollars have been received for the October180 calls than were paid for either of the other calls. Therefore, if IBM declines before expiration there will very likely be several chances to liquidate the entire spread at a profit. If the profit is sufficiently attractive when weighed against what it cost in time and money, I would accept it and look for other opportunities. This will free our capital, which might have been committed until the last Monday in October 1975.* As a trader with limited capital I prefer not to make six-month commitments in trades and would be inclined to take a profit at an early opportunity. Others may have greater financial resources and be more willing to stay longer.

* Expiration dates have been changed to the Saturday immediately following the third Friday of the maturity month.

In selecting a candidate for a butterfly spread, we should look for a combination of smallest total risk, greatest profit potential, and smallest margin requirement. No cash reserves are necessary for this position as we are covered against all price movements in the underlying stock. In general, the butterfly works best with high-priced stocks and twenty-point differentials in striking prices. This is, at present, a limiting factor in terms of the amount of money that must be put up, but we must take our opportunities where we find them.

Once we have chosen our butterfly, we are going to have certain problems with having our orders executed and reported to us without delay (unless we are exchange members). We have already discussed the difficulties of trading "spread orders" and the inadvisability of trading market orders. The same reasoning applies even more to butterfly spreads, as there is a third part of the position to trade both in positioning the spread and in liquidating it. In general, I would advise as much time as possible for taking this position and that it be completed in a single trading day. This requires getting an early start.

The maximum risk ($100 in the example given) applies to the completed position. We do not want to expose ourselves to unnecessary risk by putting on only part of the butterfly. (I suppose the name "butterfly" comes from the idea that there are two wings: the calls bought, on the outside of a denser body, the calls sold. This type of spread may also be thought of as a sandwich: the calls sold being sandwiched between the calls bought.) Naked calls sold require much more money than naked calls bought. We would like to be able to position the entire spread at close to last-sale prices for all of the parts. As we are dealing with a high-priced stock that is presumably subject to fairly broad price swings (IBM often moves several points in a day), we will have a problem getting executions close to their last sales on all of the calls. Short of executing the orders on the floor yourself, there is no foolproof way of handling this problem. I recommend a frank conversation with your customers' broker so that he or she understands the problem and your intentions. Good brokerage facilities and cooperation all along the line, from the placing of the orders to their execution on the floor, to their being reported back to you, will go a long way toward facilitating this type of order. The lack of cooperation at any point can be costly. This is part of what I meant earlier by saying that minimum margin requirements alone do not determine my choice of a broker. Attitude, executions, and reports are extremely important.

I would recommend that most people place the entire order at limit prices at the same time and ask to have the market quoted back on each part of the order. The order clerk should also be told that the order is an attempt to construct a butterfly (or liquidate one) so that he or she is in a better position to cooperate. Order clerks can be very helpful if they understand the objective, and their help may be vital.

If the two buy orders and the sell order are placed at or near last sale prices it is likely that either the buy side or the sell side will be executed. You may then find that the market is running against the executed side, in which case you will be missing the market on the other side of the spread. Perhaps the limits of your orders should allow a small fraction of leeway on both the buy and sell side. You are going to be dealing with fairly high-priced options, and eighths and quarters will have less significance. When taking this position, you should stay close to your broker, either in person or by telephone, so that you are in a position to change the limits should you miss one side of the market. We have seen that it is always safest to buy before selling and to cover shorts before selling long calls so that we are not in naked sell positions. Of course, if you have confidence in your broker, one way to handle this problem is to tell him your objective and give him the discretion to position your spread. I must confess I would probably try to improve on this (and take the risk of doing worse). To do this I would try to judge which way the stock would probably go over the next few minutes or hour of the trading day. Trying to guess this direction can be a costly business, but I will continue the attempts only until I lose more than I gain. As a clue, I would determine whether the price of gold in London had opened higher or lower. This information is available before the opening of the New York Stock Exchange. I would also ask my customers' broker to look at the previous early-morning ratio of advances to declines on the New York Stock Exchange. This is available on every quote system with which I am familiar. The market in general tends to go in a direction opposite that of appreciable moves of London gold and during a given week tends to go in the same direction as its opening on Tuesdays, Wednesdays, and Thursdays—at least for enough time to position or liquidate spreads. If *both* of these factors were in synch—for example, if London gold were more than one dollar higher and the market declines were outpacing advances—I would expect the market to continue lower in the immediate short period of the day. If I were trading on Tuesday, Wednesday, or Thursday I would, therefore, try to sell slightly under the last sale involved and try to buy for a bigger fraction less than the last sale involved, placing all of the orders at the same time and asking for quotes on each from the floor.

On Monday, if the market closed with a rally on Friday, and in the absence of important bad news over the weekend, I would expect some carryover into the first hour of trading. This might be followed by weakness, as Mondays the market closes lower than its previous close more often than any other day. I would expect to get highest prices at about 11 A.M. Eastern time and act accordingly.

If the market had been weak at the close on Friday, I would expect it to open lower, other things being equal. (I would still check London gold and the advance/decline ratio) and probably continue down. I would place my sell orders slightly under last sale prices and expect to buy later in the day at greater fractions under last sale prices.

Friday, I would expect an up day if Thursday's close was strong and I would reverse the Monday procedures. I would also watch the price movement of IBM in the expectation that the general market would follow the movement of this bellwether stock, at least for short periods of the trading day.

It must be understood that these are rough guides that I follow but can't guarantee. I don't recommend them because they are somewhat risky ° and are often counterbalanced by other factors, such as news that is constantly breaking throughout the trading day. The thoughtful reader may be able to improve on these suggestions.

In liquidating the butterfly spread it is equally important that the position be completely liquidated on the same

---

° The risk is compounded by the fact that people may abandon sound practice when such guides appear not to be working.

day, to avoid the risk of price changes in a partial position and to eliminate the need for additional margin.

How Much Does It Cost?

The minimum margin requirement of a butterfly spread is the sum of the minimum margin requirements of the two spreads into which it may be divided. In the example,

Bought 1 IBM October160 54
Sold 2 IBM October180 39½
Bought 1 IBM October200 26

the two spreads become:

1. Bought 1 IBM October160 54
   Sold 1 IBM October180 39½

This spread, with a lower striking price on the buy side, is the money only spread. Ignoring commissions, the minimum margin requirement is simply the premium of the buy side minus the premium of the sell side, or $1,450.

2. Bought 1 IBM October200 26
   Sold 1 IBM October180 39½

This spread has a higher striking price on the buy side. Its minimum margin requirement is the premium on the buy side plus the difference in striking prices minus the premium on the sell side. Again ignoring commissions, this comes to 26 plus 20 minus 39½, which equals $650.

The minimum margin requirement for the butterfly is the sum of $1,450 and $650, or $2,100.

Extra Point

It is often possible to choose a butterfly spread with a profit zone at, above, or below the market price of the stock at the time of making the commitment. In the example given, the profit zone lies below the price of the stock. This is determined by the striking price of the calls sold. If the calls sold had been the October200, the profit zone would have extended below *and* above the market price of the stock:

> Buy 1 IBM October 180 39½ °
> Sell 2 IBM October 200 26
> Buy 1 IBM October 220 16

Price of IBM at expiration of calls	*Net gain or loss of butterfly spread* °°
under $180	minus $350
$180-$200	minus $350 plus $100 per point above 180
$200	plus $1,650
$200-$220	plus $1,650 minus $100 per point above 200
$220	minus $350
above $220	minus $350

In positioning a butterfly spread, the trader may thus have an opportunity to exercise his judgment about the future price movement of a stock without being penalized in the usual way if his opinion is wrong.

° Closing prices April 2, 1975

°° Not including commissions and the SEC fee

12. Heads-You-Win, Tails-It-Doesn't-Count Spreads

We have thus far looked at five spreads that have attractive profit potentials: the time only spread; the money only spread with equal calls; the money only spread with something extra to sell; the not-only-but-also spread; and the butterfly spread. One additional spread will complete the list: the heads-you-win, tails-it-doesn't-count spread. This spread involves calls on the buy and sell sides that expire at the same time (typically, near-month maturities) and the premium differentials of which equal the *full* difference in their striking prices. Some examples of this type of spread, based on actual closing prices of April 3, 1975, include:

Buy 2 Eastman Kodak April80 at 9⅞
Sell 2 Kodak April70 at 19⅞

Buy 3 Sears April60 at 5⅞
Sell 3 Sears April50 at 16

Buy 4 Xerox April60 at 7⅜
Sell 4 Xerox April 50 at 17½

We know that as the price of the underlying stock rises, the spreads of calls of different striking prices and the same expiration widen, approaching the full difference in premiums between their striking prices. Thus, deep-*in*-the-money calls of different striking prices and the same maturity will tend to sell at premiums that reflect the *full* differential in their striking prices. The strategy with this type of spread is to buy the higher striking price calls and sell calls of a lower striking price, same expiration, when the difference in striking price is fully reflected in their premiums, as in the above examples.

The difference in premium will never widen more than a small fraction of a point beyond the difference in striking prices. Therefore, it is hard to lose much more than the commissions in this investment. On the other hand, should the price of the underlying stock decline, the spread will narrow and create a profit for us. If the stock weakens, we come out ahead; if the stock doesn't weaken, we come out about even; hence, it's a case of heads you win, tails it doesn't count.

Note that a profit is available only if the stock moves in one direction. This is contrary to the basic approach I've taken to trading. We would like to put ourselves in a position to profit regardless of market direction. However, the risk of loss here is so limited (provided we get the *full* differences in striking prices reflected in the premiums) that I think this opportunity should be considered, particularly by those who are bearish and want to eliminate the risk inherent in selling short.

What to Look for in Heads-You-Win, Tails-It-Doesn't-Count Spreads

GETTING IN

The ideal situation would involve the full striking price differential in the premium of the calls; as much time as possible; volatility of the underlying stock; an overbought market; and weakness in the underlying stock. The premium differential is simply a matter of arithmetic—either it is available or it isn't. If it isn't, we don't make the commitment. The amount of time will vary. Typically, the full premium differentials are available only in the near month. This is acceptable because the total risk is so slight, but the earlier this spread can be positioned the greater the chances for profit. Volatility is probably present or the calls would not be so deep in the money. We have seen that recent quick, sharp rises is what is meant by an overbought condition.

The last element, weakness in the stock, cannot be adequately predicted. As we have seen, we don't like to be dependent on a market move in only one direction. However, stocks that have had large upside moves often consolidate these gains by selling off somewhat. Technical reactions will create profit opportunities. In addition, the general market may be somewhat overbought. Sometimes a rally of sizable proportions occurs in a short time, followed by a "correction." Even if such reactions cannot be predicted with confidence, a further rise in the price of the underlying stock will not hurt us, as the spread cannot widen much beyond its full differential in striking prices.

What to Look *Out* for in Heads-You-Win, Tails-It-Doesn't-Count Spreads

GETTING IN

We have seen that market orders and spread orders are to be avoided and that the entire spread should be committed on the same day.

What to Look for in Heads-You-Win, Tails-It-Doesn't-Count Spreads

ALONG THE WAY

We should not liquidate only one side and stay long or short. There is no recommended opportunity for averaging. All we are concerned with is the opportunity to liquidate the spread at an acceptable profit.

What to Look *Out* for in Heads-You-Win, Tails-It-Doesn't-Count Spreads

ALONG THE WAY

We may be called for delivery. We have sold calls that are deep in the money and are therefore subject to a call at any time. If we are called, we have several choices. Let us assume we have positioned the Eastman Kodak spread above and that we are called for delivery of 200 Eastman Kodak and tendered $14,000. The premium of $1,987.50 per call is now ours to keep. If Kodak is selling above 80, we may call for delivery of 200 shares at 80, tendering $16,000 and accepting the loss of the $987.50 per call we paid for each of the Kodak80 calls. This is the way we would exercise these calls. We would then deliver the 200 shares for which we were called.

We will lose $2,000 on the exchange of stock and gain $2,000 on the liquidation (through exercise) of the calls. This is the original excess of premium which we may now keep. We would thus lose only the commissions. This is about the worst result we may expect.

If we are called for delivery and the price of the stock is above 80, we may also use the cash tendered ($14,000) with the delivery notice to go short 200 shares of Kodak in the market (we will be losing the difference between 80 and whatever the market price is but gaining an equal amount on paper on the two calls we are long). If the stock continues to move higher, we will call for delivery on the two calls we are long, tendering $16,000 in the process, and deliver them against the short position. The result will be the same as outlined above except that, in addition to the commissions, we will have to pay any dividend that is declared while we are short. The amount we have paid for the stock delivered to us is equal to the amount we got for the stock we delivered earlier, minus $2,000. But the calls that have been liquidated (by their exercise) have netted us a premium differential of $2,000. We are therefore out only the commissions and a possible dividend.

However, if the stock declines sufficiently in price, we have an opportunity for profit. Let us assume, for example, that Kodak is selling at 110 when we are called for delivery on the April70 calls we sold. We saw that we might, if we chose, call for delivery on the calls we bought and come out with the loss of commissions only. We may decide, however, to go short 200 shares, protected against further loss by any price rise in the stock (except the possible dividend payment) by the two calls we remain long. If the stock declines, let's say to a point between 110 and 80, our net position remains the same. We will lose only commissions plus a possible dividend on the short stock. If the stock declines to a price between 70 and 80, we will gain point for point on the short stock and lose point for point (or less) on the calls. This will put us in the same net position of a loss of only the commissions and a possible dividend (with perhaps a small fraction in our favor if the stock declines toward 70. As we may deduce from Figure 2, the calls will begin to lose less than point for point as the stock declines).

However, if the stock declines below 70, we will gain point for point on the short stock but lose less than point for point on the calls still long (see Figure 2). And if the stock declines below 60, we will have a ten-point gain on the short stock and cannot lose all of the 9⅞ points we paid for the calls. This will yield us a profit which will continue to mount if the stock declines further.

If we are not called for delivery, of course, any decline in the price of the stock will tend to narrow the spread and push us toward a profit.

What to Look for in Heads-You-Win, Tails-It-Doesn't Count Spreads

GETTING OUT

An acceptable profit is the objective getting out. This will require weakness in the underlying stock and judgment as to when to take the profit. As I like to take profits only, I am inclined to accept small profits and go on to new opportunities. Long-term relationships with calls are impossible as they expire over the short term. But when to take a profit is an individual choice. What is relevant in this connection is the amount of money and time required to reach the particular profit. Subjective judgments about whether the stock will continue to go down are not persuasive. If we could rely on this sort of judgment (guesses, really) we would have been millionaires long ago. It is precisely this sort of guesswork that we have tried to avoid with this method of trading.

The dollar profits possible in this type of spread are rather small. I have never positioned such a spread, and I recommend it only with the reservations stated. For confirmed bears, it is much safer than selling short. For the rest of us, it may be worth considering under the optimum conditions described. It is something like one of those clubs in the golf bag that one hardly ever uses but which can be useful under exactly the right circumstances. In this case, the right circumstances would be a prolonged bear market. Other opportunities would be less desirable, and good profits would be available with this type of position.

What to Look *Out* for in Heads-You-Win, Tails-It-Doesn't Count Spreads

GETTING OUT

It is important to liquidate the entire position on the same day, whether it is composed of calls only or calls and short stock. This avoids a move against us in a position on only one side of the market. We are protected against loss beyond commissions and a possible dividend, and we don't want any further risk.

We have already seen that market and spread orders are to be avoided and have some rough guides as to how to liquidate spreads.

How Much Does It Cost?

In the material on the butterfly spread, we have seen that a call in which the buy side has the higher striking price requires minimum margin of the premium of the buy side plus the difference in the striking price minus the premium for the calls sold.° The spread, Bought 2 EK April80 9⅞ Sold 2 EK April70 19⅞, would require $987.50 plus $1,000 minus $1,987.50 per 1/1 call. This totals zero, and as this does not meet the minimum of $250 per 1 call bought /1 call sold spread, the minimum margin requirement would $500 for the position involving 2 calls bought/ 2 calls sold.

We have now described in detail six types of spreads which I believe hold favorable profit potentials for traders. These are the only spreads I would recommend under current rules and conditions. In the next section we will look at some recommended hedges. Again, we will be taking positions on both sides of the market and accepting the benefits of time or value or wide profit zones, or some combination of these elements. It is my opinion that the recommended spreads and hedges will provide a comprehensive approach to regular profits under an extremely broad spectrum of market conditions.

° With a $250 minimum per spread

13. Writing Hedges

A financial editor recently wrote an article that tells readers what to do if they're bullish and what to do if they're bearish. This kind of advice is twaddle. The mere fact that we may think the market is headed higher or lower surely won't cause it to go that way. Even J.P. Morgan didn't have enough money to reverse a trend. What we'd really like to be able to do is to take profits whether the market goes up, down, or sidewise and, to a large extent, we can do precisely that by writing hedges. Hedge writing refers to a position in which we sell (or write, as the streetwise guys term it) one or more calls and buy "some" shares of the underlying security.* Examples of hedge writing would include the following:

Buy 50 Polaroid	Sell 1 Polaroid July 30
Buy 200 General Motors	Sell 3 General Motors April 40
Buy any number of shares of any security that has listed calls	Sell any number of calls of any striking price and any maturity of the same underlying security

---

* We will ignore commissions and any other costs in the examples in this section in order to simplify the arithmetic. All costs will be included when we look at my actual trades in a later section.

138

One of the dictionary definitions of the verb "hedge" is "to safeguard oneself from loss on a risk by making compensatory arrangements on the other side." That is the principle we use in hedge writing. The hedge involves a position on both sides of the market—buying and selling at the same time. In hedge *writing* we take a position in which we *buy stock* and *sell* one or more *calls*. In the next chapter we will look at strategies for profits in hedge *buying*. This involves a position in which we *buy* one or more *calls* and *sell* some *stock short*.

As we are going to be talking about writing calls, it might be worthwhile to look first at the four ways of doing that:

1. Completely uncovered, or naked—this involves selling one or more calls without owning or buying *any* of the underlying stock:

Buy zero shares of stock *	Sell one or more calls of any striking price, any maturity

This is clearly not a hedge, because no stock has been positioned. We have already seen why selling naked calls is never recommended. The principal reason is that the potential loss (unlimited) is far greater than the potential profit (the premium). This is an extremely unacceptable risk/reward situation, as we've seen in the discussion of spreads. And there are other complicating factors, such as possible margin calls and calls for delivery of the underlying stock, if the stock rises, that make it even worse.

---

* Any security that could be converted to the underlying stock involved, such as a warrant or a convertible bond, would also be acceptable in lieu of shares of common stock.

2. Completely covered—this involves selling one or more calls and buying an equal number of hundreds of shares of the underlying security:

Buy 300 Avon Products	Sell 3 Avon Products April 30
Buy X hundred shares of any security that has listed calls	Sell X calls of any striking price, any maturity, of the same underlying security

This is the darling of the customers' brokers, undoubtedly the most frequently recommended kind of hedge. But as we'll see, it's a poor bet and one to be avoided. The reason why a fully covered hedge should never be positioned is: it offers too much upside potential (to a price of infinity for the underlying stock) at the expense of too little downside protection (to the extent of the premium). Nature, it appears, abhors a free lunch. Too much upside protection results in too little downside protection and vice versa, as we will see.

Why is the buyer of an Avon Products April30 call willing to pay $400 for the right to buy 100 shares of the stock at $30 per share when it is currently selling at $28 per share? Essentially, he hopes that by the time this call expires, Avon will be selling substantially higher. The buyer is paying for hope and the time within which this hope may be realized. Should the stock sell for 40 before this call expires, the call would be worth at least $1,000, two and a half times what was paid for it.

In the example: Bought 300 Avon Products 28 Sold 3

Avon Products April30 4, the maximum profit would occur at the striking price of 30 for the stock on the expiration date. At $30 per share at expiration, all of the calls would be worthless and their premiums would be profit. The stock bought at 28 would also have a two-point profit. This would yield a gross profit of $1,200 for the calls (3 times $400) plus $600 of appreciation on the stock (3 times $200) for a total of $1,800 on the position.

No matter how high the stock rose above 30 at expiration the gross profit would be $1,800. Each point above 30 would yield a profit of $100 per hundred shares of stock, and this would be offset by $100 per call, as the calls would begin to take on value in direct relation to the price of the stock as it rose above 30. This is what is meant by upside protection up to infinity. At all prices above $30 for the stock, the gain on the stock would equal the loss on the calls sold.

However, on the downside, this position offers protection only to the extent of the premium. If the stock declines below 28 minus 4, to 24, the $400 premium no longer covers any further loss. If, for example, the stock were selling at 22 at expiration, the calls would be worthless for a gross profit of $1,200, the amount we got for selling them. But the stock would show a loss of $600 per hundred shares, or $1,800, for a total loss of $600.

This position has infinite protection on the upside but only 14.28 percent protection on the downside (4/28). As the stock cannot possibly sell at infinity but may certainly sell below 24 before the calls expire, we have a poor mix. This is true of all fully covered calls, and this is why I never recommend them.

3. Overcovered—this involves the selling of one or more calls and the buying of more than an equal number of hundred-share lots of the underlying stock:

Buy 500 General Electric	Sell 2 General Electric October40
Buy more than X hundred shares of the underlying security	Sell X calls of any striking price, any maturity of the same underlying stock

This, as you can see, offers infinite protection on the upside and even less downside protection than the fully covered option and is rejected even more strongly.

4. Partially covered—this position involves selling one or more calls and buying some stock but less than one hundred shares per call sold:

Buy 100 Avon Products 28	Sell 2 Avon Products April30 4
Buy X shares of the underlying security	Sell a call or calls on more than X shares of the same underlying stock, any striking price, any maturity

Writing partially covered hedges offers the best combination of profit potential and safety because we may select in advance (within limits) the profit zone as well as a number of additional factors which will increase our chances for profits on a regular basis. This is, therefore, the only type that is recommended. Let's look at an example from my own trading and see what factors go into a desirable hedge writing position.

On December 27, 1974, I took the position: Bought 100 Avon Products 28 Sold 2 Avon Products April30 4.

As we have seen, the point of maximum profit for this position would be a price of 30 for the stock at the moment the calls expired on April 28, 1975. The calls would expire worthless, and I would keep the premiums ($800). In addition, the stock would have appreciated two points for a total gross profit of $1,000.

I consider the premium of any call to be the sum of two values: its "time value" and its "point value." The point value of a call is the number of points (and fractions of a point) the underlying stock is currently selling *above or below* the striking price of the call. In the above example, Avon Products was selling at 28, 2 *points below* the striking price of the call. The point value of the April30 was therefore minus 2. The time value (which is the only other value in the call I recognize) must therefore have been 6 points in order for the call to have a premium of 4. We now have a working formula for describing the premium of any call: Premium equals point value plus time value. In this case, 4 equals minus 2 plus 6. If Avon Products rose to a price of 32 and the Avon Products April30 were selling at 6½, the point value would be 32 minus 30, or 2, and the time value would have to be 4½: 6½ equals 2 plus 4½.

Let's now look at the profit zone of the position I took. The downside of the profit zone is found by subtracting the sum of the premiums received for all of the calls sold from the total price paid for all of the stock bought and dividing by the number of hundred shares bought. The total price paid for the stock * was $2,800, the total premiums equaled $800, and the number of hundred shares bought was 1 ($2,800 minus $800 equals $2,000; $2,000 divided by 1 is $2,000). The downside of the profit zone would be the point at which the stock was selling at 20, or $2,000 for all of the stock bought.

This can be easily checked by looking at what would happen at expiration if the stock were selling at 20. The calls would be worthless, and we would gain $800. However, since we paid 28 for the stock and it is selling at 20, we have an equal and offsetting loss of $800 on 100 shares.

To find the upper limit of the profit zone we begin at the point of maximum profit, which is always the striking price of the calls at expiration. At a price of 30, as we have seen, the total profit on the position would be $1,000 at expiration. For every point above 30, we would gain $100 on the stock but lose $200 on the calls. We lose a net $100 per point (at 30) but we began with plus $1,000 at 30. Consequently, the upper limit of the profit zone is 40 at expiration of the calls.

Therefore, on December 27, 1974, with almost exactly four months until the calls expired, I could make this commitment with the knowledge that the maximum potential profit was $1,000 and the profit zone was between 20 and 40. This profit zone gave me 8 points of protection on the downside, or 28.57 percent (8 divided by 28) and 12 points of upside protection, or 42.86 percent (12 divided by 28). That is, in order for me to lose money the stock would have to lose more than 28.57 percent of its value or gain more than 42.86 percent in four months and one day. I considered this unlikely and made the commitment.

* For simplicity we are not including commissions, etc.

Use this page for your computations

Thus far we have looked at this example considering only what would happen at the expiration date of the call. However, we should not ignore what might have happened in the interval between positioning this hedge and the expiration date. Every moment that elapsed would be reducing the time value of the call. Time, as we know it, goes only in one direction. The calls continually move toward expiration, and their time values move toward zero.

It is obvious that if the price of the stock declined with the passage of time, the premiums of the calls would have to decline. However, even if the stock *rose* in price, if it did so at a slow enough rate, the premium of the calls might well decline. It might even be possible to take a profit on both the stock and the calls if the stock rose fairly slowly or if the market recognized that the premium of the calls was too high, or both. This was my objective. Within twelve days, as we'll see in detail when we examine my trades, I was able to take a profit on the stock *and* the calls, for an annualized gain of 273.75 percent, uncompounded, including commissions and other charges.

I chose to be half covered (I sold calls that would require delivery of twice as much stock as I bought) because it allowed me good protection on the downside (28.57 percent) and excellent protection on the upside (42.86 percent), where I thought I'd probably need more protection. The market had been through a withering decline. The Dow Jones Industrial Average was slightly over 600, near its low point for the past ten years. At least as important, Avon Products, which had sold at a high of 140 in 1973 and a low of 18⅝ in 1974, also seemed to have more room on the upside.

These are points to be kept in mind in deciding where to place the limits of the profit zone. All of these data are immediately available to any customers' broker. The broker may not be able to tell you how to make a profit, but he has all of these figures at his fingertips.

Let's look at some of the many mixes that were available and their corresponding profit zones:

Cover- age	Commitment	Max- imum Profit	Profit Zone	Upside Protec- tion	Down- side Protec- tion
⅔	B 200 AVP 28 S 3 AVP A30 4	$1,600	22-46	64.29%	21.43%
½	B 100 AVP 28 S 2 AVP A30 4	1,000	20-40	42.86%	28.57%
⅓	B 100 AVP 28 S 3 AVP A30 4	1,400	16-37	32.14%	42.86%

The coverage I chose required less of a cash investment than the other two examples shown. These examples, of course, do not represent the only possibilities. I could have bought 200 shares and sold 5 calls or bought 300 shares and sold 8 calls, etc. A high degree of fine tuning can be obtained by selling one call and buying an odd lot (less than 100 shares of stock); e.g., Buy 43 shares and sell 1 call, etc.

What to Look for in Writing Partially Covered Hedges

GETTING IN

1. The market price of the stock should be below the striking price of the calls sold. The point value of the calls will therefore always be negative and the buyer of the calls

will be paying for *time only*. We, as the seller of those calls, can expect the pleasurable opportunity of converting time into money in a kind of modern alchemy.

2. Sell calls with a high buyer's break-even price per week. This figure is found by dividing the number of points the stock would have to rise at expiration for the call buyer to break even by the price of the stock. This number is then divided by the number of weeks to expiration. The result is the percentage of the market price of the stock (at the time we buy it) the stock would have to rise each week if the buyer of the call were to break even at the expiration date of the calls. The higher that percentage, the less likely for the call buyer to break even and the more likely we are to profit by selling the calls.

3. A limited time until expiration of the calls. Obviously, the less time until the calls expire, the less time for the stock to trade out of the profit zone and the faster the time value of the calls should decline, other things being equal. I recommend no more than twenty weeks to maturity.

4. As high a price for the calls as possible. I recommend at least two dollars for the call, as downside gains are harder to realize when the calls are too low-priced.

5. A fairly stable stock. High volatility will work against us, causing the stock to trade out of the profit zone.

6. A wide profit zone, with additional protection on the side indicated. In the Avon Products example, I chose greater protection against an upside move in the stock because the stock was low-priced in relation to its recent price history and the market was near its low over a ten-year period. In addition, the market had just been through a prolonged and sharp decline. If Avon had been selling at 100 and the Dow Jones Industrial Average had been

hovering near 1,000 I would have elected greater downside protection, other things being equal. I would say, as a rough guide, that one-half coverage (selling calls on twice as much stock as bought) with a striking price about ten percent above the market price of the stock would be a good mix. We want to avoid selling too many excess calls, as in the case of money only spreads with something extra to sell. My own preference would range between one-half and one-third coverage. I would not recommend less than one-third coverage.

What to Look *Out* for in Writing Partially Covered Hedges

GETTING IN

1. As the stock will be selling at a higher price than the calls and therefore is subject to wider price fluctuations, I would, as a general rule, recommend buying the stock before selling the calls. However, as indicated in the material on spreads, I prefer to try to outguess the immediate price moves and obtain better prices, and risk getting clipped occasionally. Although it is permissible to trade the stock at the market, I would avoid doing so with the calls.

2. We should try to avoid oversold stocks and oversold markets. Ways of doing this were set forth in the material on time only spreads. We don't mind if the stock declines after we position this hedge, as the calls will decline significantly and give us an opportunity to cover them at a good profit. As with spreads, I look for about a 50 percent decline in premium as a satisfactory profit. Since the stock faces no expiration date, we don't mind early declines. A

sharp rise in the price of the stock, however, can bring a demand for delivery of stock on calls sold and complicate the position.

3. We should avoid positioning too many excess calls. The reasoning is the same as that applied in the case of money only spreads with something extra to sell. (That section should be reviewed.) Less than one-third coverage is uncomfortable and increases the psychological pressure on any rally in the stock.

What to Look For in Writing Partially Covered Hedges

ALONG THE WAY

Writing hedges is much like positioning money only spreads with something extra to sell. Not surprisingly, much of the same reasoning applies. What to look for along the way involves the same considerations in both cases. The first objective is an acceptable net profit on the entire position. If that does not present itself, I look for an acceptable net profit on the calls sold. Fifty percent of the premium received would ordinarily be acceptable. I would then look for a small profit on the stock. Please review this material in the section on money only spreads with something extra to sell.

What to Look *Out* for in Writing Partially Covered Hedges

ALONG THE WAY

The same considerations would apply here as were set forth in money only spreads with something extra to sell. To repeat, I believe that the preservation of capital is of great importance. If losses are strictly limited, we always have the opportunity for later profits. Therefore, I think the wisest course in this position is to narrow the profit zone to include commissions and other costs plus a small surplus for missed markets and bad executions. When the stock reaches the upper or lower limit of the new profit zone, I recommend liquidating the position. You may occasionally take a loss, but the loss will be small and you may even have a profit. In order for the stock to trade out of the adjusted profit zone, it must make a fairly sizable percentage move. (If this were not the case, you wouldn't have made the commitment.) A fairly sizable move, particularly for a stock that is not volatile, takes a certain amount of time. The more time it takes, the less time value remains in the calls sold. Near-month out-of-the-money calls go into an accelerated decline as they approach expiration, as we saw in Figure 1. If the calls go into the money, they tend to sell close to their point values. That is to say, there is little or no additional premium for time only. Thus the longer it takes for the stock to move to the upper limit of the profit zone, the greater the chance for profit.

The same is true for the lower limit, for the calls will be approaching zero. If this is not entirely clear to you, it should become apparent when we look at actual examples in my own trading account.

If the stock rises sufficiently we may be called for delivery of 100 shares of stock per call sold. Unlike the commodity markets, in which short sellers may be called for delivery only in the month in which the contract expires, writers of calls may be required to deliver at any time. If you have followed the suggestions and are called for delivery, you will be in the adjusted profit zone.

With the exception of an occasional opportunity for an

arbitrage by a stock or options exchange member, most calls for delivery will occur close to the expiration of the call. There is no point in tying up cash to take delivery of stock. The floor arbitrage occurs when there is a chance to sell the stock short and buy the call at a profit, exclusive of commissions. In such a case, a member (who does not have to pay commissions) may do so and call for delivery of the stock against the call. For example, if Avon Products were selling at 36 and the April30 call were only 5¾, this opportunity for a risk-free small profit would occur. This sort of arbitraging would quickly narrow the profit to a point where the opportunity would no longer exist.

A more typical example of a call for delivery would be Avon Products at 35, for example, three weeks before expiration of the calls, with the calls selling at 5¾. The entire position could be liquidated at a $350 profit (minus commissions, etc.) The stock, which was bought at 28, at 35 would show a gross profit of $700; the two calls, bought at 5¾ and sold at 4, would show a gross loss of $350.

However, let us assume that you were trying for a bigger profit when you were called for delivery of 200 shares of the stock and given $6,000. You might deliver the 100 shares bought at 28, keep $3,000, and also keep the $400 premium for one of the calls. This would yield a gross profit of $600 for the stock and one of the calls.

You would have a choice with respect to delivery of the second 100 shares. You might buy 100 shares at 35 and deliver it. This would cost $3,500 but you would keep the $400 for the call plus the $3,000 that accompanied the delivery notice. This would create a loss of $100, which, subtracted from the $600 profit on the first 100 shares delivered, would yield a profit of $500.

If you were convinced the Avon Products was overpriced at 35, you might have delivered 100 shares and have gone short the other 100 shares, hoping to cover the short position at a lower price, but trying to outguess the market is not recommended.

If called for only 100 shares, I would recommend delivering the 100 shares originally bought and liquidating the other call by buying 1 Avon Products April30 at 5¾. This would create a loss of $175 on the second call to be subtracted from the $600 profit, for a total profit of $425. There are tax consequences and strategies in this kind of transaction that will be examined in the section on taxes.

In the above example, I probably would not have been called because I would most probably have liquidated the entire position at a profit before that point had been reached. I prefer to take reasonable profits as quickly as possible and go on to the next opportunity, turning over and increasing my capital.

What to Look for in Partially Covered Hedges

GETTING OUT

If the limits of the adjusted profit zone have been observed, and the position has been selected in accordance with all of the suggestions outlined above, there is an excellent chance that the only thing to look for getting out will be an acceptable profit. There is one additional possibility that should be considered. If the calls decline to 50 percent of the premium originally received, I would be inclined to liquidate them. If there were an acceptable profit on the entire position at that time, I would not hesitate to take it. But if the profit were minimal, I might hold the stock for a profit. I am extremely careful about this move for it is a position that will yield a profit only if the market goes one way—up—and that is what I try to avoid. One way to handle this position is to cover all of the excess calls at a profit and stay long—a hedge in which you are fully covered.

In the above example, if Avon Products were selling at 28½ a month later and the Avon Products April30 calls were selling at 2, I would probably liquidate the entire position. But one call could be covered at a profit of $200 and the fully covered position held. A new profit zone would have as its lower limit the breakeven point (including commissions and all costs) of the new position. The upper limit is infinity as any price above 30 for the stock would yield a $600 gross profit. Covering the excess calls releases cash in the account, plus the profit. The new position would be held until an acceptable profit presented itself or the stock touched the lower limit of the new profit zone. A call for delivery would simply require delivery of the stock positioned.

What to Look *Out* for in Partially Covered Hedges

GETTING OUT

Avoid market orders in liquidating the calls.

How Much Does It Cost?

In figuring the minimum amount of money to be put up in writing partially covered hedges, the position is treated as if it were composed of two parts: Part I, a fully covered hedge and Part II, one or more naked calls. In the example given:

Use this page for your computations

Bought 100 Avon Products at 28
Sold 2 Avon Products April30 at 4

Part I is
Bought 100 Avon Products at 28
Sold 1 Avon Products April30 at 4

Part II is

Sold 1 Avon Products April30 at 4

Part I, the fully covered hedge, requires the amount needed for the stock minus the amount received for the call. The current minimum requirement for the stock is 50 percent (plus the commission) and the amount received for the one call is $400 (minus a commission and a 1¢ SEC fee). Ignoring the commissions and the fee, Part I would require 50 percent of $2,800 or $1,400 minus $400 or $1,000.

As we saw in the case of money only spreads with something extra to sell, the naked call (Part II) requires a minimum of 30 percent of the market price of the underlying stock minus the difference between the striking price of the call and the market price of the stock times $100 minus the net proceeds of the call. Ignoring commissions, Part II would require 30 percent of $2,800 or $840 minus $200 (30 minus 28 times $100) minus $400 or $240. However, as we saw, there is a minimum requirement of $250 for each naked call.

Part I requires $1,000; Part II requires $250, and the minimum sum needed would therefore be $1,250.

14. Buying Hedges

We have, up to now, examined the various strategies and tactics for buying (getting in), holding (along the way), and selling (getting out) seven recommended positions: time only spreads; money only spreads with equal calls; money only spreads with something extra to sell; not-only-but-also spreads (money and time); butterfly spreads; heads-you-win, tails-it-doesn't-count spreads; and writing hedges.

One additional position offers sufficient opportunities for profit, under certain conditions, to be worth considering. This position, which I call buying a hedge, involves the purchase of one or more calls and the short sale of an equal number of hundreds of shares of the underlying stock. Some examples of buying hedges would include:

Buy 1 IBM July200 Sell 100 IBM short
Buy 5 Upjohn April45 Sell 500 Upjohn short
Buy 2 Gillette January 30 Sell 200 Gillette short
Buy 4 Eastman Kodak October100 Sell 400 Eastman Kodak short

Selling short involves the sale of a stock you do not own with the hope of buying it back later at a lower price. Your

157

broker will borrow the stock for you and deliver it to the buyer to whom you sold it. Your account is thus short of that stock, and you will, at a future time, be required to deliver the number of shares you are short. Should you be able to buy this stock at a sufficiently lower price (to cover more than commissions and the other costs, plus any dividends that may have accrued to the buyer while you were short), you will have a profit. If not, you will have a loss.

There are times when a call is selling at a premium that has a zero time value. In other words, the striking price of the call plus its premium is approximately equal to or less than the market price of the stock. On April 18, 1975, for example, Kerr McGee closed at 79¼, the Kerr McGee April65 closed at 14, and the April75 closed at 4⅜.

Let us assume that we sold 100 shares of Kerr McGee short at 79¼ and bought 1 Kerr McGee April75 at 4⅜. Ignoring commissions and other costs for the moment, if Kerr McGee stayed at the same price or rose, we could exercise our call before it expired and deliver, against our short position, the 100 shares we would thus obtain at 75, liquidating the position at a loss of ⅛ minus all costs of the trades. This is the worst that could happen on the upside, plus the payment of any dividend that may have accrued to the buyer.

However, if the stock declined in price, we might have an opportunity to profit. If the stock fell eight points prior to the expiration of the call, for example, we could buy 100 shares and deliver them against our short position, closing it out at an eight-point profit. Since the call cost only 4⅜, it cannot decline eight points. We might either sell the call, adding to our profit, or keep it for a free ride, hoping the stock would rally prior to the expiration of the call.

The basis of our profit is a decline in the price of the stock, and we are protected from a loss of more than commissions (and a possible dividend) if the stock does not decline. For every point the stock drops, we gain a point on it. But the premium of the calls will tend to decline less than a full point for each point the stock loses (see Figure 2). And, of course, the call cannot decline more points than we paid for it, nor can it decline as much as the stock since the stock is higher priced. If the stock should decline more points than we paid for the call, we have an opportunity for two profits: covering the stock and selling the call (liquidating the entire position); or covering the stock and keeping the call for a possible rally in the stock. If the stock rallies, the premium of the call will rise.

The ideal hedge would include all of these factors:

1. As much time as possible and at least six weeks until the calls expire—the more time, the greater opportunity for the stock to decline enough to give us a profit (and a possible free ride on the call).

2. Little or no time value in the premium of the call. This limits the risk to only the costs of the transactions (commissions, etc.). In the example:

Sold 100 Kerr McGee short at 79¼
Bought 1 Kerr McGee April75 at 4⅜

exercising the call would require putting up 75 times $100 or $7,500. Thus, for $7,500, plus the price of the call of $437.50 we could get 100 shares of Kerr McGee, which is worth $7,925. We are paying only ⅛ of a point ($12.50) for the time value, a small price indeed. The time value of a call may be calculated by adding its striking price to its premium and subtracting the market price of the underlying stock.

3. As low a price for the call as possible and not more than 10 percent of the price of the stock. The lower the price of the call, the better chance for a free ride; i.e., the stock has to decline the number of points we paid for the call (plus costs) to give us a chance to buy back the stock at a profit which equals the price we paid for the call, insuring us against loss and allowing us, if we wish, to hold the call for a possible rise in its value or to sell it at once, adding to our profit in either case. The smaller the number of points the stock has to decline to accomplish this, the more likely it is to occur.

4. A volatile stock. Price stability works against us by using up time.

5. An overbought stock in an overbought market—the weaker the stock, the better.

6. No dividend to pay on the stock until the expiration of the call. The short seller pays the dividend but the call buyer doesn't get it. This is a minor point.

Getting in, it is advisable to sell the stock short before buying the call. The stock is higher priced and subject to greater price variation. In addition, short sales are subject to the uptick rule, originally introduced to prevent raiding stocks and forcing their prices lower. Stocks may be sold short only at a price that is higher than the previous *different* price. Thus, if the stock declines in a straight line, it may not be sold short. If you've bought the call first, you are losing part of the premium you paid without any

Using some actual examples from *The Wall Street Journal* or other source, try to calculate a few time values.

corresponding gain in the stock. Calls are not subject to the uptick rule at the present time.

Along the way, I look for an opportunity to either liquidate the entire position at a profit or, even better, to get as close to a free ride on the call as I can for as long as I can.

Getting out, I don't recommend market orders. If I were liquidating the entire position, I would be inclined to cover the stock before selling the call, but would want to do both on the same day. An early start and cooperation from one's customers' broker and staff are helpful.

How Much Does It Cost?

Minimum margin requirements for this position are high. The call bought must be paid for fully. In addition, the minimum margin requirements for positioning the short stock are added to the full purchase price of the call. In the example given: Bought 1 Kerr McGee April75 4⅜ Sold 100 Kerr McGee 79¼ short, the minimum margin requirement (exclusive of commissions) would be $437.50 for the call plus $3,962.50 (50 percent of the value of the stock is the current minimum margin requirement for selling stock short)—a total of $4,400.

This position requires a considerable cash investment relative to its profit potential and has limited potential: a profit will result only if the market moves in one direction. These are serious drawbacks, and I have never positioned this hedge. However, in overbought markets and during major bear swings this position would serve as a vehicle for gains, while limiting the possibilities of loss.

We have now seen eight positions that can be used to

create profits during periods when the market is rising, flat, or falling. I don't recommend any other positions. There may be some people who can sell naked calls or take other ill-advised positions and make a killing, and good luck to them. Some people also clean up at Las Vegas! Even a bad investment may occasionally show a profit, but high-risk ventures are unlikely to yield steady profits, and they usually place one under a great strain. Wall Streeters often quote the "greater fool theory," which states that it is all right to make a foolish investment if you can find a bigger fool willing to make a worse one by taking you out at a profit. I don't subscribe to this: greater fools have a way of being in short supply when they are most needed. I prefer to rely on the elements of time, value, a broad profit zone, and strict limitation of risk at the time I take the position, rather than to look for fools later.

The next section details my own voyage of discovery in trading listed calls. We will see the method evolving under actual playing conditions. I will point out a number of pitfalls and other obstacles I didn't see at first and had to overcome. I strongly advise readers not to rush into trading until, at an absolute minimum, they have read and understood this material and the Options Clearing Corporation prospectus and have experimented on paper to their own satisfaction. At that time, for those who want to go forward, I would suggest that trading be commenced on a very small scale.

15. To Have and Have Not

The subject of taxes is an extremely complex one. The sheer bulk of tax codes and court decisions is forbidding, and there is a continuing process of interpreting, amending, distinguishing, proposing, revising, overruling, remanding, and ignoring. A lay person soon finds himself beyond his depth in what has become a highly specialized area. And if you make a mistake or fail to meet a deadline, there may be heavy penalties. I have three degrees, including a law degree from an Ivy League law school, but I have to hire professional services to compute my own income tax returns. I could do it myself, but the difference between a barely competent job and a highly professional one has become so great that there is a net savings in both money and time which I can otherwise use productively if I pay for professional excellence. Or, at least, that's what I tell myself. We've come a long way from Thoreau's life style; maybe too long.

At any rate, I'm not going to attempt to give specific advice on taxes; I'm not qualified to do that. However, I think it is important to raise some of the issues, for we all know that what you net from what you get is of crucial importance.

What makes the tax consequences of listed options transactions particularly uncertain is the fact that there have so far been few court decisions. In addition, some of the basic terms are being defined in contradictory ways in different places. For example, a listed call option is a "security" for some purposes but is not treated as a security for other purposes. And the tax consequences of gains and losses for listed call buyers and writers, or sellers, of the same options are sometimes dramatically different.

It would be easy to duck the entire subject by suggesting that individuals should consult their own tax advisors before entering into options transactions. I have seen the problem treated that way many times. I endorse that general view, but I think individuals should become a little better prepared to discuss the issues with their tax advisors so that the advice is more to the point and perhaps less expensive for having saved some of the expert's time.

Even as a non-expert, I can see several anomalies in the current tax laws, and I believe there will be changes written into the law. Some of these changes may render obsolete a certain amount of the material in this section. But the basic principles will probably stand for some time, and we must approach the subject from where we find ourselves. Here, then, with all of the appropriate disclaimers flying, is my understanding of the current tax consequences of trading in listed options, and some of the possible strategies for keeping the legal maximum of your profits.

Let us look first at the tax treatment accorded the buyer (or holder) of a listed call option. Gains or losses for the call buyer are capital gains or losses. And the length of the holding period (whether or not it is more than six months) determines whether the capital gain or loss is long- or short-term. Long-term capital gains are given favorable tax treatment. For example, the first $50,000 of long-term capital gains ($25,000 if you are married and file a separate return) may be reduced by 50 percent and then taxed at the regular rates; or, you may elect to pay a flat 25 percent on long-term capital gains if this is more advantageous. Taxpayers with long-term capital gains in excess of $50,000 ($25,000 if married and filing a separate return) who use the above alternative may have to pay up to a maximum of 35 percent of their long-term gains in excess of this break point.

Calls bought, which expire unexercised after they are held more than six months, result in long-term capital losses. Should the calls expire unexercised six months or less after they are bought, the premium and commission are short-term capital losses.

Calls that are exercised have the effect of adding the premium of the call (plus commission) to the cost of the stock. The holding period of the stock determines whether its subsequent sale results in a long- or short-term capital gain or loss. Note that it is only the holding period of the *stock*, not the holding period of the call and not the holding period of the call plus the holding period of the stock, that determines whether the capital gain or loss is long- or short-term.

Under the present tax rules, if the call buyer has a long-term capital gain on a call, he will lose the long-term status of the gain if he exercises the call and buys the underlying stock. He will defer the payment of any tax by exercising the call (until he sells the stock at a gain), but the premium and commission paid for the call are added to the price of the stock for tax purposes, and the holding period for capital gains treatment begins with the date on which the call is *exercised,* not the date when the call was *bought.* Thus, the underlying security, the *stock,* must be held for more than six months to give him a long-term capital gain opportunity. Therefore, assuming tax considerations are important to him, if the call buyer doesn't intend to hold the underlying security as a long-term investment (and doesn't expect to be in an appreciably lower tax bracket when he does sell the underlying security) he should sell the call before it expires and take a long-term capital gain.

After taking a long-term gain on the call, he may, if he chooses, buy the stock at once in the market. His over-all income and capital gain or loss position, plus, perhaps, his estimate of his income and capital gain or loss position for the following year, will play an important part in his decision.

Different considerations apply to the writer of listed calls. The Internal Revenue Service (IRS) has taken the position that the writer of a listed call has not conveyed an asset because the writer may close out his obligation in a closing transaction at any time he chooses, provided he has not received an exercise notice and the call has not expired. Therefore, gains to writers of listed calls who either allow the calls to expire unexercised or who buy in the calls they've written in closing transactions are considered to be ordinary income and not capital gains. There are some, including myself, who think writers of listed call options should be treated the same as short sellers of warrants and that the gains or losses should be treated as capital gains or losses, not additions or subtractions to or from ordinary income, but this is not the case at present.

Thus, if a $5,000 gain, for example, is realized by

writing calls and closing them out or letting them expire unexercised, the $5,000 is added to ordinary income and taxed accordingly. And a $5,000 short-term loss on options bought could not be used to offset this gain. The individual would have to pay taxes on the $5,000 gain at the full rates for ordinary income and would be allowed to deduct only a total of $1,000 per year against ordinary income for the $5,000 loss, assuming he had no other capital losses to offset.

If the call is exercised against the writer and the writer has to deliver stock, the price received (striking price minus the costs of the transactions) is increased by the premium received (less the costs of the transaction). The transaction gives rise to a capital gain or loss, which will be long- or short-term, depending upon the holding period of the stock. If the call has been written against long stock purchased prior to the exercise of the call written, and if the stock has been held more than six months, the gain or loss will be considered long-term. If the stock bought for delivery has been held six months or less, the gain or loss will be considered short-term. The premium is not taxable until expiration, exercise, or a closing transaction occurs.

These rulings and interpretations give rise to a number of possible ways of converting ordinary income to capital gains and short-term gains to long-term gains. (The latter are taxed at lower rates.)

Purchase of stock and sale of deep-in-the-money options may yield capital gains and losses of ordinary income. For example, with Eastman Kodak at 95, we may buy 100 EK 95 and Sell 1 July60 36½. If Kodak remains above 60, which is very likely if we have sold a nearest-term call, we have a choice.

1. If Kodak is between 60 and 95, wait for an exercise notice and take a small net short-term gain.

2. If Kodak is above 96½ (and the call has not been exercised against us), we may buy in the call in a closing transaction and take a loss against income. We may then either take a short-term capital gain in the stock by selling it or try to convert that short-term capital gain into a long-term capital gain (with much safety) by selling a deep-in-the-money call with an expiration date more than six months after the purchase date of the stock. If we have a gain in the stock after six months and a loss in the call, we may then take a long-term gain on the stock and an income loss on the call. If there is a profit in the call, we wait to receive an exercise notice and take a long-term gain and no loss of income.

Let us look at some other strategies available to the option writer under current tax interpretations. As the courts have not yet spoken on most of these considerations, it is particularly necessary to discuss your specific plans with your own tax advisor.

Let us suppose you have a position that includes long 100 Avon Products at 28 and you've sold (or written) 2 Avon Products April30 at 4. Let us further assume that after you have held the stock at least six months and one day, with the stock at 36, you have an $800 long-term gain on the stock, and the calls—at a price of 6½—show a paper loss of $500, excluding commissions. Prior to receiving an exercise notice on the calls written, you may decide to close out the position.

Selling the stock at 36 results in a long-term gain of $800; buying in the 2 calls at 6½ results in an income loss of $500. If you were, for example, in the 50 percent tax bracket, your long-term gain would net you $400, while your income loss would save you $250. If you multiply that illustration sufficiently, you could eliminate your entire income and have no tax to pay other than long-term capital gains taxes. This is an opportunity to get long-term capital gains while receiving a potential deduction from income.

In a rising market, this works very well for the writer of calls. However, in a falling market, it works against the writer. The gain on the calls written is considered ordinary income, while the loss on the stock is considered capital loss and is deductible from income only at the rate of $1,000 per year (assuming there are no other capital losses against which to offset it).

In a position involving calls long against calls short (spreads), if the market rises, you may have an opportunity to take long-term capital gains and deduct the losses from ordinary income. For example, if you are long 10 EK April70 and short 10 EK April80 and the stock rises, let us say, to 100, your gain on the EK April70 (which will actually exceed your loss on the April80) will be long- or short-term capital gain, depending on the length of time you held the calls. The loss on the EK April80 may be deducted from your income. However, if the price of the stock fell, your loss on the EK April70 would be a capital loss, while your gain on the EK April80 would be added to your ordinary income.*

---

* The C.B.O.E. has an 18-page pamphlet entitled "Tax Considerations in Using CBOE Options." It was prepared by a firm of Certified Public Accountants and it provides a useful guide to the subject. The C.B.O.E. offers it at no cost or it may be available through your broker.

16. The Bottom Line

As mentioned in Chapter 2, on April 23, 1975, less than five months from the November 26, 1974 starting date, I had achieved the goal set for this book: 51 profits without a single loss. Although I think this record is excellent, my total gains were sharply limited by a number of factors. First, the need to take so many profits in so limited a time forced the acceptance of a profit almost the moment one appeared. The requirement that I could not take a loss cost much time which could have been saved by taking a small loss, allowing funds to be committed to better advantage. The splitting of our total available capital into three accounts meant that occasionally a trade could not be made because, although the three accounts together had enough funds to position it, no single account did. (The pension, profit sharing, and our own joint account were required by law to be separate.) Dividing the funds into three accounts also meant smaller positions in any single account and therefore higher commissions. In addition, and this factor will be discussed in greater detail in the next chapter, a number of problems, which should not have occurred, arose with my broker and were hampering.

With only about $8,000 divided between two accounts

and less than $1,500 in free cash in another account, which was used only during the last two and one-half months, I owned or controlled 24,400 shares of stock with an aggregate value of more than $1 million. Even if these figures are halved, as I was almost always on both sides of the market, I think the methods set forth in this book got a fair testing. With all of the limitations imposed and after commissions, state taxes, SEC fees, and interest to the broker, the profits amounted to $7,620.98 in less than five months. The 45 consecutive profits in the profit and pension accounts totaled $6,806.68 in less than five months, a rate of profit of 13.1 percent *compounded monthly*, an annualized gain of 338 percent. The six consecutive profits in the other small account netted more than 61 percent in two and one-half months, a gain of 21 percent, *compounded monthly*, an 885 percent annual gain.

For the record, the following summary includes every closed transaction made in the three accounts in which I traded throughout the period shown. Not a single one has been added, subtracted, concealed, abridged, adulterated, omitted, or misstated:

THE PROFIT SHARING ACCOUNT

	Trade date	Trade	Commission	State tax	SEC fee	Net amount	Gain
1.	11/26/74	S 1 Upjohn A50 7	$25.00	$	$.02	$ 674.98	$
	1/ 9/75	B 1 Upjohn A50 3	25.00			325.00	349.98
2.	11/26/74	B 100 Polaroid 22 3/8	48.82			2286.32	
	2/20/75	S 100 Polaroid 23 1/2	50.55	5.00	.05	2294.40	8.08
3.	11/26/74	S 1 Polaroid A25 3 3/4	25.00		.01	349.99	
	1/31/75	B 1 Polaroid A25 3/4	6.30			81.30	268.69
4.	12/ 4/74	B 1 Eastman Kodak A70 5 7/8	25.00			612.50	
	1/ 9/75	B 1 Eastman Kodak A70 3 1/4	25.00			350.00	
	1/10/75	S 2 Eastman Kodak A70 5 1/8	37.33		.03	987.64	25.14
5.	12/ 4/74	S 3 Eastman Kodak A80 3 3/4	44.63		.03	1080.34	
	12/27/74	B 3 Eastman Kodak A80 1 7/8	37.31			599.81	480.53
6.	12/ 6/74	B 1 Xerox J50 9 3/4	25.00			1000.00	
	1/ 3/75	S 1 Xerox J50 11	26.30		.03	1073.67	73.67
7.	12/ 6/74	B 100 Reichhold Chemicals 10 5/8	30.66			1093.16	
	1/13/75	S 100 Reichhold Chemicals 11	32.59	3.75	.03	1151.13	57.97
8.	12/31/74	S 3 Xerox A70 1 13/16	37.07		.02	506.66	
	1/15/75	B 2 Xerox A70 1 1/4	27.25			277.25	60.52
9.	12/31/74	B 1 Xerox A60 3 3/4	25.00			400.00	
	1/29/75	B 1 Xerox A70 3 7/8	25.00			412.50	
	1/29/75	S 1 Xerox A60 9	25.00		.02	874.98	231.37
10.	1/ 2/75	B 100 Northwest Airlines 12 1/2	33.57			1283.57	
	1/27/75	S 100 Northwest Airlines 13 1/2	35.11	3.75	.03	1311.11	27.54
11.	1/ 2/75	S 2 Northwest Airlines J15 1 7/8	28.88		.01	346.11	
	1/15/75	B 2 Northwest Airlines J15 1 7/16	27.74			315.24	30.87
12.	1/15/75	B 1 Upjohn J45 4 1/2	25.00			475.00	
	2/ 3/75	B 4 Upjohn J45 2 1/8	47.05			897.05	
	2/12/75	S 5 Upjohn J45 2 7/8	60.69		.03	1376.78	4.73
13.	1/29/75	B 2 Upjohn J45 2	29.20			429.20	
	4/18/75	S 2 Upjohn J45 4 3/8	24.76 *		.02	850.22	421.02

* Commission lower as part of larger order

THE PROFIT SHARING ACCOUNT (continued)

	Trade date	Trade	Commission	State tax	SEC fee	Net amount	Gain
14.	1/13/75	B 1 Upjohn J45 7	$25.00	$	$	$ 725.00	$
	2/26/75	B 3 Upjohn J45 2 1/4	38.78			713.78	
	3/ 5/75	B 3 Upjohn J45 1 1/2	35.85			485.85	
	3/17/75	S 7 Upjohn J45 3 3/8	84.71		.05	2277.74	353.11
15.	1/15/75	B 1 IBM J160 22 1/2	41.25			2291.25	
	1/15/75	S 1 IBM J180 14 1/2	30.85		.03	1419.12	
	1/29/75	B 1 IBM J180 21	39.30			2139.30	
	1/29/75	S 1 IBM J160 31 3/8	50.24		.07	3087.19	75.76
16.	1/15/75	B 1 Eastman Kodak J70 6	25.00			625.00	
	1/15/75	S 2 Eastman Kodak J80 3 3/4	33.75		.02	716.23	
	1/16/75	B 1 Eastman Kodak J70 6	25.00			625.00	
	1/31/75	S 2 Eastman Kodak J70 8	44.80		.04	1555.16	
	1/31/75	B 2 Eastman Kodak J80 4 1/4	35.05			885.05	136.34
17.	1/28/75	S 1 IBM J160 33 1/4	51.93		.07	3273.00	
	1/28/75	B 1 IBM J160 31 1/4	50.13			3175.13	97.87
18.	2/ 3/75	S 4 Upjohn J50 1 1/4	42.50		.01	457.49	
	3/ 5/75	B 4 Upjohn J50 7/8	29.40			379.40	78.09
19.	2/20/75	B 50 Polaroid 20	27.32			1027.32	
	2/26/75	S 50 Polaroid 21 3/4	28.67	2.50	.03	1056.30	28.98
20.	3/ 3/75	S 3 Upjohn A45 3/4	18.90		.01	206.09	
	3/ 5/75	B 3 Upjohn A45 7/16	11.03			142.28	63.81
21.	3/ 7/75	S 7 Upjohn A45 9/16	33.08		.01	360.66	
	4/ 1/75	B 7 Upjohn A45 7/16	25.73			331.98	28.68
22.	3/ 6/75	S 3 Upjohn A50 3/16	4.73		.01	51.51	
	4/16/75	B 3 Upjohn A50 1/16	1.58			20.33	31.18
23.	3/17/75	B 7 Upjohn J45 3 3/4	87.63			2712.63	
	4/18/75	S 7 Upjohn J45 4 3/8	86.68 *		.07	2975.75	263.12
24.	3/18/75	B 2 Polaroid 025 5·3/8	37.98			1112.98	
	4/23/75	S 2 Polaroid 025 7 3/4	44.15		.04	1505.81	392.83

* Commission lower as part of larger order

THE PENSION TRUST ACCOUNT

	Trade date	Trade	Com-mis-sion	State tax	SEC fee	Net amount	Gain
25.	12/ 4/74	S 3 Eastman Kodak A80 4	$45.60	$	$.03	$1154.37	$
	12/24/74	B 3 Eastman Kodak A80 1 15/16	37.56			618.81	535.56
26.	12/ 4/74	B 1 Eastman Kodak A70 6 1/2	25.00			675.00	
	1/31/75	S 1 Eastman Kodak A70 7 1/8	25.00		.02	687.48	12.48
27.	12/27/74	B 100 Avon Products 28	56.07			2856.07	
	1/ 7/75	S 100 Avon Products 30 3/4	59.01	5.00	.07	3010.92	154.85
28.	12/27/74	S 2 Avon Products A30 4	34.40		.02	765.58	
	1/ 8/75	B 2 Avon Products A30 3 5/8	33.43			758.43	7.15
29.	12/30/74	B 300 Warner Comm. C pfd 2	37.07			637.07	
	1/14/75	S 300 Warner Comm. C pfd 2 3/8	39.75	3.75	.02	668.98	31.91
30.	12/30/74	S 1 Polaroid A25 1 3/4	25.00		.01	149.99	
	1/31/75	B 1 Polaroid A25 3/4	6.30			81.30	68.69
31.	12/30/74	B 1 Polaroid A20 2 3/4	25.00			300.00	
	1/17/75	B 1 Polaroid A20 1 3/8	25.00			162.50	
	1/31/75	S 2 Polaroid A20 2 1/2	30.50		.01	469.49	6.99
32.	1/ 9/75	B 1 Eastman Kodak A70 3 1/4	25.00			350.00	
	1/14/75	B 1 Eastman Kodak A70 3 3/4	25.00			400.00	
	1/28/75	S 2 Eastman Kodak A70 4 1/4	35.05		.02	814.93	64.93
33.	2/ 5/75	S 2 Polaroid A25 1 3/8	27.58		.01	247.41	
	3/ 5/75	B 2 Polaroid A25 1 1/16	20.77 *			233.27	14.14
34.	2/ 4/75	S 2 Polaroid A25 1 5/16	27.41		.01	235.08	
	3/ 5/75	B 2 Polaroid A25 1 1/16	20.76 *			233.26	1.82
35.	2/ 4/74	B 100 Polaroid 20 1/2	45.92			2095.92	
	2/12/75	S 100 Polaroid 22 7/8	49.58	5.00	.05	2232.87	136.95
36.	2/20/75	B 50 Polaroid 20	27.32			1027.32	
	2/26/75	S 50 Polaroid 21 3/4	28.67	2.50	.03	1056.30	28.98
37.	3/ 5/75	S 3 Kennecott A35 2 3/4	40.73		.02	784.25	
	3/12/75	B 3 Kennecott A35 1 5/8	36.34			523.84	260.41

* Commission lower as part of larger order

THE PENSION TRUST ACCOUNT (continued)

	Trade date	Trade	Commission	State tax	SEC fee	Net amount	Gain
38.	3/ 5/75	B 3 Kennecott J40 2 1/8	$38.29	$	$	$ 675.79	$
	4/21/75	S 3 Kennecott J40 2 3/4	40.73		.02	784.25	108.46
39.	3/ 5/75	B 4 Upjohn J45 1 1/2	43.80			643.80	
	4/18/75	S 4 Upjohn J45 4 3/8	58.75		.04	1691.21	1047.41
40.	3/ 6/75	S 3 Upjohn A50 3/16	4.73		.01	51.51	
	4/16/75	B 3 Upjohn A50 1/16	1.58			20.33	31.18
41.	3/ 7/75	S 1 Upjohn A45 9/16	4.73		.01	51.51	
	4/ 1/75	B 1 Upjohn A45 7/16	3.68			47.43	4.08
42.	3/13/75	S 3 Kennecott A40 3/8	9.45		.01	103.04	
	4/21/75	B 3 Kennecott A40 1/4	6.30			81.30	21.74
43.	3/18/75	B 2 Polaroid 025 5 3/8	37.98			1112.98	
	4/23/75	S 2 Polaroid 025 7 3/4	44.15		.04	1505.81	392.83
44.	4/22/75	S 2 Polaroid J25 8 5/8	46.43		.04	1678.53	
	4/23/75	B 2 Polaroid J25 6 7/8	31.70 *			1406.70	271.83
45.	4/23/75	B 4 Polaroid J25 6 7/8	63.43 *			2813.43	
	4/22/75	S 4 Polaroid J25 7 1/4	72.10		.06	2827.84	14.41

CHARELL JOINT ACCOUNT

	Trade date	Trade	Commission	State tax	SEC fee	Net amount	Gain
46.	2/ 7/75	S 2 Polaroid A25 1 1/8	26.93		.01	198.06	
	3/11/75	B 2 Polaroid A25 3/4	12.60			162.60	35.46
47.	3/ 6/75	S 2 Kennecott A35 2 3/8	30.18		.01	444.81	
	3/12/75	B 2 Kennecott A35 1 3/8	27.58			302.58	142.23
48.	3/ 6/75	S 2 Upjohn A50 3/16	3.15		.01	34.34	
	4/16/75	B 2 Upjohn A50 1/16	1.05			13.55	20.79
49.	3/ 6/75	B 2 Kennecott J40 2	29.20			429.20	
	4/21/75	S 2 Kennecott J40 2 3/4	31.15		.02	518.83	89.63
50.	3/ 6/75	B 2 Upjohn J45 1 1/2	27.90			327.90	
	4/18/75	S 2 Upjohn J45 4 3/8	35.38		.02	839.60	511.70
51.	3/13/75	S 2 Kennecott A40 1/4	6.30		.01	68.69	
	4/21/75	B 2 Kennecott A40 3/8	4.20			54.20	14.49

* Commission lower as part of larger order

PROFIT SUMMARY

November 26, 1974—April 23, 1975

45 gross trading profits		$10,268.75
(profit sharing and pension trust accounts)		
Dividends	+	56.00
Commissions	−	3,419.28
State taxes	−	31.25
SEC fees	−	1.34
Interest	−	66.20
(equals)	$	6,806.68

February 7, 1975—April 21, 1975

6 gross trading profits		$ 1,050.00
(Charell joint account)		
Dividends		0.00
Commissions	−	235.62
State taxes		0.00
SEC fees	−	.08
Interest		0.00
(equals)	$	814.30
Total profits:	$	7,620.98

17. The Good, the Bad, and the Ugly

So far, we have been looking for the most part at the sunny side: the high profit potential that options trading offers, and my trading record and methods. Now, in fairness to readers, it is incumbent upon me to present a balanced picture of the environment in which options are traded.

The "bad" aspects include a lack of competence with options among many registered representatives (customers' brokers) and back-office personnel and a lack of sufficient concern about this on the part of management; a relatively long trade-to-tape time on the C.B.O.E.; and a financial daily press that publishes closing prices but fails to publish the daily ranges of options.

I found all of these shortcomings hampering. The 51 consecutive profits I took involved 114 purchase and sale confirmations. Too many of these contained at least one error. Three of the errors were commission overcharges. For each of these overcharges it was I, not the firm, who initiated the request that the correction be made. How many other customers are being overcharged without their knowledge and without reimbursement?

The brokerage house I dealt with is a member firm of unquestioned reputation and great stature, not some bucket shop. The lesson is clear: knowledge and vigilance are required. In the words of fight announcers: "Protect yourself at all times." This requires a knowledge of the rules and a willingness to check all confirmations, statements, and other communications from brokers. It doesn't take much time to do this and it's necessary.

Errors on purchases and sale confirmations are clear-cut and hard to deny, as are overcharges of commissions. However, there are damaging acts or omissions inflicted upon brokerage customers that are less obvious and often undetected.

It is, for example, usually impossible for a customer to know that a needless delay has caused him to miss the market, to his detriment. Many brokers do not yet know the symbols for the various options and they have to look them up each time, which wastes time. Ineptness on the part of the customers' broker, further delays in getting the order to the order clerk, delays by the order clerk, the floor clerk, the broker on the floor, or others, can easily result in loss to customers. Carelessness, indifference, and lack of competence may all play a part.

High volume of trading also typically overloads the capacity of back-office personnel. In the past I was able to receive a written confirmation of a trade the following morning. Now it sometimes takes two or more days, even if there is no error in the confirmation that might delay it further.

There is, at present, an abysmal lack of expertise about listed options on the part of even highly paid and impressively titled brokerage personnel. Margin clerks are not thoroughly familiar with the margin rules that govern listed options accounts so you may expect to receive erroneous margin calls. Even so-called options specialists in some firms, who are receiving six-figure annual salaries, are unfamiliar with the finer points of the rules. With greater familiarity this situation should begin to change soon.

In the meantime, brokers, aware of their own lack of expertise in listed options, have moved swiftly to protect not the customers but themselves. In what should be recognized as a prizewinner of creative nerve, they have attempted to foist upon customers the concept of no-recourse negligence. Customers are being required to sign options agreements that include the following clause: "You [the broker] shall not be liable in connection with the execution, handling, selling, purchasing, exercising, or endorsing of puts or calls for my account, except for *gross* ° negligence or *willful misconduct* ° on your part."

Try to prove either. And your proving may be made a bit more difficult because the same agreement contains the following clause: "In the event of any dispute between us or claim by me or claim by you on account of the purchase, sale, handling, execution, or endorsement of puts or calls for my account, the same shall be arbitrated in accordance with the rules of the exchange on which the put or call which is subject of the dispute is traded or in accordance with the rules of the New York Stock Exchange, Inc., if the put or call is not traded on a national securities exchange."

That may sound fair, but a few caveats about the arbitration procedures are in order. The C.B.O.E. says a non-member may request arbitration "in accordance with the rules." The procedure is to file a written statement with

° Emphasis added, of course

the Secretary of the Exchange. A copy of the written statement requesting arbitration (containing the allegations and other material), the reply of the member, any counterclaim the member may file, and any reply to the counterclaim are all sent to the parties concerned and then returned to the Secretary. The Secretary then submits the papers to the Arbitration Committee with a copy to the Chairman of the Board. The Board or the Arbitration Committee "may decline in any case to accept a submission for arbitration." If not so declined, the Arbitration Committee "shall assign the matter to a panel of arbitrators. . ."

The Arbitration Commiteee "shall consist of at least nine members of the Exchange or persons registered as option Principals, none of whom shall be a director of the Exchange or the Clearing Corporation." The Chairman, with the Board's approval, "shall from time to time appoint a panel or panels of non-member arbitrators consisting of persons who are not engaged in the securities or commodities business."

A non-member may elect to have the panel of arbitrators composed solely of members of the Arbitration Committee. Otherwise, the panel of arbitrators will consist of "two members of the Arbitration Committee and three non-members selected from the non-member panel" as described above.

I would prefer to seek my remedy in a different forum—if necessary, in the courts. Juries are made up of one's peers, not of colleagues of the party against whom you have a grievance. I recommend not waiving your right to select the proper forum in which to have your grievance heard. This requires that you not sign any agreement with a broker that requires you to submit all disputes to arbitration. If you are presented with such forms that waive these and/or other rights, read them carefully before signing them. If you have any question or doubt, consult your own legal advisor. I recommend simply crossing out, in ink with neatly ruled lines, those passages in the forms which you find disagreeable and returning the signed forms. If the amended forms are unacceptable to the broker, I would look for another broker after voicing my objections. After all, if arbitration, for example, is so attractive, why shouldn't you have the right to voluntarily select it?

I see no point in limiting my rights in this way. If enough people did this, perhaps the brokers would become more responsive and responsible.

However, it *is* possible to find competence, accountability, and responsibility among brokers and it is hoped that with the passage of time and greater experience gained with listed options more and more firms and their personnel will be included in this number.

18. Winning

Successful options trading requires a disciplined approach. It should not be entered into casually, for it is a serious undertaking and the pitfalls, for the unwary, are many. The first question to be considered is that of personal suitability; i.e., is options trading a proper area of endeavor for a particular individual? Trading in a rapidly shifting marketplace involves risk taking, which may not be suitable for many people. Age, experience, financial position, income, future earning capacity, temperament, health, responsibilities, and other individual differences should be factored into the decision. Trading in options is certainly not for everybody. And what might be suitable for an individual at a particular time may not be suitable for the same individual at another time under other circumstances. If you are in doubt, I would suggest staying out of the options markets.

Should you decide to trade in options, I believe that the methods and techniques set forth in these pages provide a sensible approach to making profits under the existing rules and conditions. I've backed that belief with my own funds and am still doing so.

In this section I would like to provide a number of additional aids that, strictly speaking, lie outside a method of trading but are properly a part of a profitable course of trading. These aids are the results of my own personal experience in trading securities for my own account for more than twenty years, nine years of which were spent in the securities business, where I had the opportunity to closely observe the way my clients, and the clients of colleagues, invested and traded in the securities markets.

Enthusiasm is a wonderful quality, highly prized and, alas, too rarely found among adults. But overenthusiasm and the false confidence that lead to rash and financially damaging errors should be avoided. The best way I know to avoid such losses is to begin to apply these trading methods on paper, risk-free. There is no need for hasty action. You must prepare yourself for the long pull if you hope to come out ahead. The markets will be open for business next week and next year. Use the same care in practicing that you would exercise if you were using actual cash, and keep accurate records of all trading, including commissions. Only when you are able to take paper profits consistently should you begin to risk a penny of actual cash.

The next hurdle is the choice of a registered representative or customers' broker. A good registered representative for handling stocks and bonds is not necessarily the right choice to handle your options trading (although if a customers' broker had not been good with your stocks and bonds, there is little chance that he will do a satisfactory job with options). There is a wide range of competence among registered representatives in handling options trading. Some competent registered representatives have simply never learned the mechanics of the options markets, and member firms and others have not done all they should have to educate their employees, both back-office and registered personnel.

As, essentially, I am not seeking advice from a customers' broker, I look for competence in handling orders, knowledge of the rules and procedures involved in options and a desire to keep abreast of changes in them; punctuality during market hours; the accessibility of the individual (if the telephone lines are always busy, I can't place orders); adequate coverage during lunch hours and at other times the person may be away from the desk; honesty; the ability and the inclination to get broker errors corrected (erroneous margin calls, missed markets, errors in reports and commissions, interest charges, etc.); and a desire to be of service. A final requirement is the clarity of thought and language that separates a representative who can provide a valuable service from one who can cost you thousands of dollars and untold nervous strain and not even be aware of it.

Another extremely important area to consider is the financial condition of the firm and its willingness to be responsible for its errors. Any prospective customer has the right to ask for a current balance sheet of a brokerage firm with which he is considering doing business. In addition to determining the liquidity and financial strength of the firm, check to make sure your account would be insured up to $50,000 in securities and up to $20,000 in cash should the firm become insolvent or go out of business, and whether there would be any limitation on that insurance other than the maximum amounts stated above.

Margin requirements should be considered. Check the minimum equity required of an options account as well as the original margin and maintenance requirements. These requirements vary widely, both among member firms as well as between member firms and non-member firms. Also determine what margin is required of the "naked calls" part of hedges.

Interest rates on debit balances also vary from firm to firm and among accounts in the same firm. Ask for preferred rates, based on the size *and/or* the activity of your account. Even small options-trading accounts generate good commissions for the firms, and your knowledge of this fact can save you money. You won't get a preference for activity unless you ask for it, in my experience.

Try to determine the excellence of executions from employees of the firm as well as from their customers. Be sure to visit the brokerage office and ask questions. Get a first-hand feel of the place. If you don't like it you are under no obligation to open an account.

Those brokerage firms that ask options accounts to sign what they call an options agreement are, in effect, requiring the customer to underwrite the firm's negligence. The account is asked to agree that the firm shall not be liable in trading options except for gross negligence or willful misconduct. Apparently, ordinary negligence that damages the customer doesn't count. I have a natural tendency to expect that firms which try to shirk their responsibilities for negligence (the ordinary kind, not gross) must have something to worry about; I would take my business elsewhere unless there were compelling reasons that attracted me to the firm, and then I would try to have the agreement modified.

Commission schedules also vary. Determine in advance what commissions the firm charges. Find out the rate for options whose premiums are under a dollar, which are ordinarily not published with the rest of the commissions schedule. Think of the difference in commissions in terms of the volume of trading you contemplate. But I repeat, it is penny-wise to save a few dollars per year in commissions and lose sight of other factors that are much more important to the success of your trading. Other things being equal, of course, dollars saved are dollars saved.

An ideal broker in an ideal brokerage firm may not exist. Certainly, I haven't found one. In deciding upon a customers' broker and a firm, find the best mix for you. The various factors may be weighed differently by different individuals, depending on their needs and circumstances. What is important is that you should be satisfied. And if and when you become dissatisfied with the performance level, you should exercise your right to find another situation that is more to your liking—the sooner the better.

When you're ready to trade with actual coin of the realm, *begin on a small scale*. This will ensure that early mistakes will be made at as low a cost as possible. If there is a price to be exacted for actual experience, it will pay to keep it to a minimum. You will have to deposit a minimum amount in order to sell calls, but you need only use a portion of the minimum deposit for any small position you may wish to take.

Enter the market only after deliberation: never on hope or hunch. Always protect your position from big losses. The strict, sensible limitation of loss will provide the opportunity for a comeback. Limit your risk on any one position. Divide your trading capital into several bundles and don't commit more than one bundle to an original position. It may later become necessary to "rescue" the position by averaging down or taking other corrective action suggested in the sections on trading strategies, and within the limits suggested, this is recommended. But limit your original commitment to prevent serious loss. Don't overcommit your funds and don't overtrade. As you build your trading capital by taking profits, resist the temptation to pyramid your gains into bigger and bigger individual commitments. While it is all right to engage in *more* positions as your capital grows, it is a mistake to keep plowing back every gain into *larger and larger* positions. Taking more positions with the increased funds keeps the odds constant or even slightly alters them in your favor. But "doubling up" makes any single loss a big one. It is permissible to gradually increase your positions, but draw down some cash reserves as a reward for having been right.

The *patience* to hatch a good profit is desirable, and the patience to wait for a good opportunity is essential. My profits were much too small and should not be used as a model. As pointed out, I took such tiny profits in order to run up the score of consecutive profits as part of a contractual obligation for this book, and against the book's deadline. Since you don't have this problem, go for good trading profits. Avoid scalping the market for minuscule gains. I have indicated the guidelines I think are practical in the various trading strategies.

Profit by learning from your mistakes. Analyze any losses; look for the cause, write it down in your own words, keep it handy, and then don't make that mistake ever again. Experience is an excellent teacher, but only if accompanied by awareness and a good memory.

Don't let a profit become a loss. Speculation and preservation of capital are often thought of as being mutually exclusive. It is conventional to think that low risk and low reward go together as do high risk and high reward. It is clear to me that there are exceptions to this concept, and my objective in trading in the listed options markets is to reduce risks and exposure as much as I reasonably can while keeping potential rewards high.

Avoid joint decisions. If you have to pool your funds with those of somebody else to enter the market, don't do it. Wait until you can do so with your own money. The markets require the consistent application of judgment. If you have to consult with the other party, you will lose flexibility, and you will almost inevitably miss many markets. Even if you have total carte blanche to make all decisions, your judgment will be influenced in subtle ways by the fact that you will feel called upon to explain or account for your decisions. I have seen this mistake made many times, and made it myself many years ago.

Keep your perspective. If you find that options trading consumes too much of your time or energies or keeps you awake at night, pass it by. If you find your disposition mirrors your trading results; i.e., if you are all smiles when you take a profit but scream at those closest to you when you take losses, take the pressure off your life and hang it up. This is not your game—pass and be well.

If you are not enthusiastic about a potential investment or trade, don't make it. Avoid 55/45 situations; 95/5 is where the profits lie.

Keep your funds handy, but don't commit them until you're ready. I use a day-of-deposit to day-of-withdrawal savings account for this purpose, and I keep the account in a convenient bank where I can use the money any day I choose to do so. Banking by mail to get the last eighth of a percent interest has its virtues, but I give that up for the convenience of getting the use of the funds the day I need them. Options trades must be settled on the day following the purchase or sale. Definitely use a separate account for your trading funds. Don't commingle these funds with any others, because you may be tempted to dissipate them on other than investment objectives. I keep my investment funds intact, well protected from being nibbled to death by ducks.

Protect yourself at all times. All of the trading strategies herein provide limitation of exposure, and there are other built-in safeguards. Use all of these procedures for limiting your exposure to loss. Don't buck the trends. Don't try to prove something to the market, the market makers, your customers' broker, your friends or to anybody else, including yourself. Don't become ego-involved with your positions. If you are wrong, a small loss is better than a big one. The market isn't wrong if you are sitting with a loss, you are, so face it and avoid running an error into a full-scale debacle. A small loss is little enough price to pay for being wrong once in a while.

Check everything, and the sooner the better. Take nothing for granted. People make mistakes and so do machines. Remember those scenes in the old Westerns in which the old wrangler puts the promising kid up on the horse and the kid promptly falls right on his face because the old wrangler deliberately failed to buckle the saddle on? The point was that the kid should have checked the saddle himself. This applies to brokers, too. Check every term of every confirmation. The number of errors is surprising in view of all of the sophisticated machinery used. Get the highs and lows of the day on the securities you've traded that day. The financial press is inadequate; I don't know of a single daily newspaper that now supplies the range for options. Ask your customers' broker. You may find, as I have, that you've paid more than the high of the day or gotten less than the low. The sooner these errors are perceived, the more easily they are corrected.

Good health and good spirits are important. At least two or three times a year it is a good idea to close out all positions and take a rest from the market. Clear your head and get a better perspective.

When you decide to make a trade, if you follow the methods and the techniques set forth in the various trading strategies and if you adhere to the practical suggestions in this chapter, I believe you will have excellent chances to get ahead of the game and stay there. And one final suggestion: if you find that you are not ahead after trying options trading, don't force it. There are some highly intelligent people who are simply not cut out to be options traders. The only proper course for these people is to realize this is not their game.

19. Help!

When I was in the fourth grade a big card was hung above the blackboard which read: "KNOWLEDGE IS POWER." None of us questioned the weighty motto, and even today I think we could find general agreement that information has a big edge over ignorance. It is a recommended practice, before indulging in games involving play money, that we at least familiarize ourselves with the rules of the game. Should this be any less necessary when playing for real money?

Fortunately, there are a number of simple and inexpensive ways to add to knowledge about listed options trading and to improve our performance. Every exchange on which options trade puts out informational booklets on the subject, and they are usually free and easily obtained either directly from the exchange or through a broker. I would certainly get recent copies of the prospectuses and all of the other relevant material available at no cost from the exchanges and/or from brokers. Also recommended are the booklets setting out the options rules on each particular exchange. In addition, I would spend five dollars on the "Chicago Board Options Exchange Constitution and Rules." I would also ask to use whatever library facilities my broker had, and if I saw a reference item that looked worthwhile I would buy it. A public library with a financial section would serve the same function.

A few hours with these materials will soon make you much more knowledgeable than the average customers' broker as well as the so-called options specialists and a good many floor officials as well, if my experience is typical.

Once you have acquired this important background, it helps to stay current. I subscribe to *The Wall Street Journal* and read *Barron's* every week, not so much to find valuable information that I can use directly but in order to learn what everybody else is finding out. Making money in securities markets is a little like "choosing" (the variation I used to play as a child involved two players who, at a given signal, extended either one or two fingers of one hand; if both players extended the same number of fingers, the player who had elected "evens" won; if not, the point went to the "odds" player). If your analysis is too far ahead of the field, you won't make any money right away and you may even lose. The idea is to stay one move ahead. In choosing, if you "outthink" the opponent by one move, you will win, but if you "outthink" him by two moves, you will lose.

The Wall Street Journal is widely read in the financial community, and it really takes very little time to utilize it in a systematic way. The second column on the front page briefly summarizes the important business and financial stories; the next to last page has two columns called "Abreast of the Market" and "Heard on the Street" that should be read. The rest of the paper may be scanned for headlines (including the small headlines). This takes about ten minutes a day. If you have additional time, the front-page articles are recommended and, of course, any story that interests you can be clipped for reading in down time the same day. *Barron's*, a weekly publication, provides among many other features an excellent statistical rundown of the various markets.

If you become serious about options trading and do so on a fairly large scale, in addition to a membership or clearing privileges that may be looked into, there are services that may become worthwhile. There are, for example, stock quotation services that are available for a monthly charge plus telephone costs—some may be bought outright instead of rented. These services provide quotes on stocks (on a delayed basis, but the options prices are actual, last sales). The various exchanges can tell you which services carry their options prices. Both *Barron's* and *The Wall Street Journal* carry occasional advertisements for these services, and you may wish to send for the free descriptive material. I have never used these services for two reasons: I didn't want to have an advantage not available to the general public in establishing my profitable record of trading, and they would have added too much to the cost of my trading in relation to its scale. If I'd been trading more actively, and with more funds, I might have bought this sort of service.

There are also cable television systems in certain localities that include the New York Stock Exchange and American Stock Exchange tickers and other financial data on some of their channels. This sort of service can be useful in following the immediate trends of the markets. However, the systems all have a delay (usually fifteen minutes) which means that you are watching the prices your broker saw on his tickers fifteen minutes earlier.

Some people prefer to watch the tickers in their

broker's office. My own preference is to avoid brokerage offices as much as possible. They are places where people are subject to mob psychology. Hopes and fears and guesses and rumors are often treated as facts, and they are magnified as they ripple through the assembled tape watchers. This is not a place for calm deliberation. Tape watching tends to make us impart too much significance to a few trades, and when done in a group, it is easy to lose perspective. You're better off never hearing the uninformed opinions that are offered in brokerage firm board rooms.

20. The End

For nine years, a couple of careers ago, I was a member of the so-called financial community. I've traded my share of blue chips, cats and dogs, hot issues, bullion, municipal bonds, bags of silver coins, potatoes, and investment securities, as principal and agent, for myself and hundreds of clients. I became convinced that the public had the worst of it over the long haul, despite some exceptions and a number of favorable short-term swings. It was this opinion, slowly formed over a period of years, that led me to leave the retail side of the securities business; at a substantial personal cost I terminated a long-term business relationship for which I no longer had enthusiasm.

The new listed options markets, however, offer a number of innovative potentials. I have demonstrated, at least to my own satisfaction, that relatively high rates of return are available within acceptable limits of risk. Most of the strategies in these pages are based on my own firsthand experience, and you have seen my trading record. I believe the methods set forth in these pages present a sensible approach to trading listed options. Spreads and hedges, positioned, held, and closed out in accordance with the suggested approaches, also reduce the psychological stresses associated with high-risk ventures.

My primary consideration has been to try to limit the

risks as much as possible while keeping the profit potential high. Perhaps Willy Loman's brother Ben summed it up best: "The jungle is dark but full of diamonds. . . ." It is my hope that the approaches suggested provide light and surer footing.

Glossary

The following glossary explains the technical terms used in this book:

averaging down   buying an additional quantity of a security at a lower price than was paid for the previous lot, thus lowering the average unit cost

bear market   a general market condition in which the prevailing direction of securities prices is toward lower prices

bull market   a general market condition in which the prevailing direction of securities prices is toward higher prices

butterfly spread   a position that consists of selling two calls and buying one call of higher striking price and one call of lower striking price on the same underlying security, all of which expire at the same time

buying a hedge   a position that consists of one or more calls purchased and the short sale of some shares of the same underlying security

199

call an option to buy a designated security at a stated price for a specified period of time

call for delivery notice requiring the seller of a call to deliver stock at the striking price

cash account a customer account in which positions must be paid for fully in cash

clearing member a member of an exchange that has joined the Options Clearing Corporation

closing price the price at which the last sale of the day was transacted

closing transaction the liquidation (or partial liquidation) of a position; it involves buying in, or covering, a shorted security or selling long a security previously purchased

completely covered a position that involves the selling of one or more calls and the buying of an equal number of hundreds of shares of the underlying security

completely uncovered a position that involves one or more options bought or sold with no offsetting position in the underlying security; also known as naked

correction a short, minor move in the market or in a particular security or industry group which is counter to the major trend *coverage* the extent to which a position involving one or more options sold includes a purchase of the same underlying security

covering liquidating a short position with an offsetting purchase

day order an order that expires, if unexecuted, at the end of the trading day

deep in-the-money option an option whose striking price is more than five points less than the market price of the underlying stock

deep out-of-the-money option an option whose striking price is more than five points above the market price of the underlying stock

exchange minimum the smallest amount of equity required to establish (or maintain) a position, as set by the particular exchange on which the security or securities in the position are traded. (House minimums are almost invariably higher than exchange minimums.)

exercise to acquire the underlying security by the timely submission of an exercise notice to the Clearing Corporation by the Clearing Member acting on behalf of the exercising option holder (see "call for delivery")

exercise price the price per share at which call options may be converted to the underlying stock by the holder of the call and at which the holder of a put may require payment per share for the underlying security; also known as the striking price

expiration date   the last day on which an option may be exercised

heads-you-win, tails-it-doesn't-count spread   a spread that involves calls on the buy and sell sides that expire at the same time (typically, near-month maturities) and on which the premium differentials equal the full difference in their striking prices

hedge   a position that involves the purchase of a security and sale of one or more options in the same underlying security, or vice versa

house minimums   the smallest amount of equity required by the firm with which the account is held to establish (or maintain) a position

in-the-money option   an option whose striking price is lower than the market price of its underlying stock

last sale   the price at which a unit of trading was last transacted

leverage   the use of a relatively small sum to control an asset of considerably greater market value, so that a small price change in the asset of greater value causes a relatively greater price change in the asset positioned

limit order   an order to purchase or sell a security which specifies the lowest price the seller is willing to take or the highest price the buyer will pay

limited risk   a position in which the maximum loss is calculable and a safeguard is in place which protects the position from any further loss

liquidate   a closing transaction in which a position is exchanged for cash

liquidity   the extent to which a position may readily be converted to cash; this is a function of the "size" of the market

long   that part of a position which includes an opening purchase transaction

maintenance call   a request for more collateral in order to bring the account up to the house minimum-equity requirements

margin   funds or securities having loan value deposited against an open position in a margin account

margin account   a type of securities account in which positions may be taken without the requirement that they be paid for in full; the precise amounts that may be borrowed are prescribed by federal, exchange, and house rules *margin call*   a request for collateral; an original margin call requires an amount necessary to position a commitment; a maintenance call requires an amount needed to hold a position that has gone against an account

market maker   one of the competing specialists on the floor of an Exchange (C.B.O.E., for example) who has an obligation to help maintain a fair and orderly market in a specific option or options

market order   an order to purchase or sell a security at the best available price at the time the order reaches the trading floor; the best available price may be the offered price in the case of a market buy order and the bid price in the case of a market sell order

marking to the market   to maintain sufficient collateral in a margin account, brokers revalue positions on the basis of current prices; should the market have moved sufficiently against a position, a maintenance call may be issued; by the same token, should the market favor a position with unrealized gains, marking to the market will create additional buying power or make cash available to be withdrawn

maturity   the date an option expires; often referred to simply by the month of expiration

member firm   a brokerage firm that has one or more seats on an exchange, although the term has been widely used to indicate firms that are members of the New York Stock Exchange

minimum variation the smallest price change of a security; lower priced options (selling under two or three dollars on U.S. options exchanges) have minimum variations of one-sixteenth of a dollar; options with higher premiums have one-eighth of a dollar minimum variations

mix the ratio of calls sold to hundreds of shares of stock purchased in a hedge, or the ratio of calls sold to calls bought in a spread

money only spread a spread that involves calls on the buy side on which the terms differ from the terms of an equal number of calls on the sell side only in their striking prices

money only spread with something extra to sell money only spread with more calls sold than bought

naked see "completely uncovered"

not-only-but-also spread a spread that involves the buying and selling of calls on the same underlying stock which are different not only in time (expiration date) but also in money (striking price)

open interest the total number of options contracts that

remain to be settled; as it takes both an original purchase transaction and an original sale transaction to create an open interest of one (options) contract, the open interest is equal to the total number of long positions or short positions in the market at a given time

open order   an order that will remain available for execution until it is canceled or executed

opening transaction   an initial purchase or sale that establishes a position in an option or options

option (listed)   a put or a call traded on an exchange which gives the holder the right to buy the number of shares or other units of the underlying security covered by the option contract from the Clearing Corporation at the stated exercise price at any time prior to its expiration (call); or the similar right to sell the number of shares or other units of the underlying security covered by the option contract (put)

option writing   selling an option in an opening transaction

Options Clearing Corporation   the Clearing Corporation is the issuer of the options covered by the Options Clearing Corporation prospectus; the Corporation is obligated to perform upon the exercise of an option in accordance with its by-laws and rules and its agreements with the exchanges; and it also serves as the clearing house for options transactions. Its principal office is located at 141 West Jackson Boulevard, Chicago, Ill. 60604

option ticker symbols

LISTED OPTION EXPIRATION CODE

Calls	Month	Puts
A	Jan.	M
B	Feb.	N
C	Mar.	O
D	Apr.	P
E	May	Q
F	June	R
G	July	S
H	Aug.	T
I	Sept.	U
J	Oct.	V
K	Nov.	W
L	Dec.	X

LISTED OPTION STRIKE PRICE

Codes	Exercise Price		
A	5	105	205
B	10	110	210
C	15	115	215
D	20	120	220
E	25	125	225
F	30	130	230
G	35	135	235
H	40	140	240
I	45	145	245
J	50	150	250

LISTED OPTION STRIKE PRICE (continued)

Codes	Exercise Price		
K	55	155	255
L	60	160	260
M	65	165	265
N	70	170	270
O	75	175	275
P	80	180	280
Q	85	185	285
R	90	190	290
S	95	195	295
T	100	200	300

original margin   the amount of cash or loan value of marginable securities needed to cover a new position

out-of-the-money option   an option on which the striking price is higher than the market price of its underlying stock

overbought   a technical condition of a market in which prices have risen too far, too fast; this term may be used in reference to the market generally, to a group of securities, or to an individual security

overcovered option   a position that involves the selling of one or more calls and the buying of more than an equal number of hundred-share lots of the underlying stock

oversold a technical condition of a market in which prices have fallen too far, too fast; this may apply to the market generally, to a group of securities, or to an individual security

partially covered a position that involves selling one or more calls and buying less than one hundred shares per call sold

premium the sum of money paid for an option by the buyer; this sum (minus commissions and an SEC fee) is kept by the seller whether or not the option is exercised

profit zone the range of prices for the underlying security which will yield a profit for a written hedge at maturity

prospectus a report describing an offering; in this context, a reference to The Options Clearing Corporation prospectus, filed with the Securities and Exchange Commission in Washington, D.C.

put an option to sell designated property at a stated price for a specified period of time

put and call brokers and dealers members of the Put and Call Brokers and Dealers Association, Inc. that formerly dealt exclusively in unlisted options contracts, guaranteed by member firms of the New York Stock Exchange

quote the highest price bid for a security and the lowest price at which it is offered at any given moment

registered representative also known as a customers' broker; an employee of a brokerage firm who has taken and passed the requirements set forth by an appropriate regulatory body for handling customer accounts

risk/reward ratio the relation between the potential loss and the potential profit

seat a membership on an exchange

selling short an opening sale transaction; selling a security without having previously bought it

SEC fee a charge on all securities sold, in the amount of 1¢ per $500 involved in the transaction (or fraction thereof)

shorting see "selling short"

size the number of trading units being bid for and offered at any particular moment; it is an indication of liquidity—that is, how many units of trading may be bought or sold at a given time and price

special option an unlisted option offered out of the inventory of a broker or dealer

specialist a member of an exchange who is charged with the responsibility of maintaining a fair and orderly market in those securities in which he "specializes"; the specialist system of making markets is used by the Amex Options Exchange

spread 1. a position in which one or more options involving the same underlying security are both bought and sold and in which the options bought differ in striking price or expiration date, or both, from the options sold. 2. the difference between the bid and the offered price of a security

spread order an order to position a spread, the buy and sell sides of which must be executed at the same time

stability the extent to which a security tends to maintain its market price

stop limit order an order to buy (or sell) a security at a price higher (or lower, in the case of a sell order) than the last sale, which becomes activated when the last sale becomes the price indicated on the order (or passes this limit), at which time the order is treated as an ordinary limit order

stop order an order that becomes a market order when its price is reached or passed

straddle a combination of a put and a call on the same underlying security at the same striking price and the same expiration date; either or both sides may be exercised at any time until expiration

strap a combination of two calls and a put on the same underlying security at the same striking price and the

same expiration date; any of the three options involved
may be exercised at any time until expiration

striking price see "exercise price"

strip a combination of two puts and a call on the same
underlying security at the same striking price and the
same expiration date; any of the three options involved
may be exercised at any time until expiration

suitability a concept that describes whether and to what
extent options trading is a prudent and proper form of
investment for a given individual, and if so, how much
trading should be conducted

time only spread a spread in which the terms of the calls
bought and the calls sold differ only in the time of
expiration. The number of calls bought and sold is equal

time value that part of the premium or price of a call paid
for the time remaining until its expiration and the
possibilities for profit that time can produce; it is
computed by subtracting the market price of the
underlying stock from the striking price of the call and
adding this amount to the premium of the call

underlying stock or security the stock that a call option
buyer has a right to receive on a valid exercise of the
call and which the put seller must tender to the buyer of
the put

unit of trading   the smallest full lot of a security that trades on an exchange

uptick   a price for a security higher than its last different price

uptick rule   the requirement that in order to sell a listed security short on a national exchange (other than options), its price has to be higher than the last different price

volatility   the extent to which a security tends to have wide price variations; also known as beta

warrant   an option to buy a security at a stated price for a specified length of time, issued by the corporation that creates the underlying security

writing a hedge   positioning a hedge in which one or more calls are sold (written) and some shares of the underlying stock are bought

writing an option   see "option writing"